*In memory of my father and mother,
you will never be forgotten.*

*To the children born in England of Jamaican parentage to give
them an authentic history of growing up in Jamaica in my era,
and to all who came to live in London after 1963.*

*Lastly, to all who desire to read a book which puts a smile on
their face.*

I was born in Jamaica, in the 1930s, in the rural area of the parish of Westmoreland. I am the last of ten children. My mother's name was Frances. Aunt Fan as she was lovingly called by everyone. My father's name was Adolphus. Uncle Dolly or Mass Dall as he was called. The family bungalow consisted of two bedrooms, living and dining room and veranda. The kitchen was a small building with thatched roof, a few yards away from the bungalow. There was an outside toilet. Opposite the veranda was a built-up area which was cemented over. This area was used for the purpose of drying coffee beans and coco beans. It was also used for drying pimento seeds. At the entrance to the gate was a tangerine tree, which produced whopping great fruits. As a child I enjoyed climbing up into this fruit tree, and just sat, quite comfortable, and ate fruits to my heart's content! Occasionally, I was forced to make a hasty retreat, due to the fact that the tree was occupied by green lizards, which would get "quite angry" having to share their "home". They would change colour from a lovely bright green to a dirty black colour. They would also look angrily at me with a sharp raised comb-like fin which ran down their back! When this happens, watch out! They are in no mood for joking! I would slither down the tree very fast! There were two rows of stones, packed neatly together, and covered in a white substance which was called whitewash. These ran down either side of the walkway, which leads from the entrance gate up to the steps to the veranda. To the right of the walkway was a beautiful flower garden, which was lovingly cared for, mostly by my elder brother, sister, and I. The house was surrounded by approximately six acres of well-fruited land.

It was situated about five minutes' walk from the main road. There were two options of getting to the main road. By walking down a dirt road, which was maintained by the residents, mainly by my dad and my older brothers, or by climbing over a stone wall, and walking through my neighbour's property. I mostly opted for the latter, as that was a beautiful estate with lots of fruit trees, and friendly grazing cows. I would usually pause and admire the large navel oranges, and on most occasions would quickly pluck one from the tree!

My first recognition of myself, and the world about me, was quite dramatic! I can remember the incident, as clear in my mind's eye, as though it were yesterday! I remember my father and my mother arguing, because my mother gave me some milk from a feeding bottle that my nephew had not finished. My father shouted at my mother, "Don't give my child milk that half dead boy drink and leave." My nephew was the first child of one of my senior sister's. She left home because she could not get along with my dad because he was too much of a disciplinarian. She went away to work as a housemaid to a wealthy headmaster in Savanna-la-Mar, the capital of Westmoreland. While she worked there she became pregnant. She had the baby and sent it home to my mother in a shoe box because it was so small! Needless-to-say, she could not return home! My father would not have her back. My mother took care of the baby. He was a very slow developer. He walked, and began to say a few words at approximately 4 years of age. He spoke with a stammer. Children called him Dummy!

The second thing that I remember, I must have been approximately 5 years of age. That same sister sent me a pair of white leather shoes. It had cross-over straps which buckled to the side. It had low heels, and leather soles. This was the first pair of shoes that I remember wearing. I am not saying that was the first pair of shoes that I had worn, but that was the one I remember and, of course, it was very unique to me. That pair of white shoes was my pride and joy! I would clean them with a kind of white stuff, which went all over my hands, and then I would put them out in the sun on the barbeque alongside the coffee beans, coco beans and pimento grains to dry! I was much amused to listen to the sound made by my shoes as I walked along the stoney roads! Of course, in those days, proper roads were only found in the towns! I would look forward to Sunday, which was the day when I would walk the two miles to Sunday-school! I could hardly wait to hear the noise made by my shoes as I walked along the stoney road!

My mother was a devoted Christian. An officer in the Salvation Army, where I attended Sunday-school, along with my elder brother and sister. Sunday's were very special to me. Mother would wake early, make breakfast, then she would bath me and comb my hair, usually she would tie the plaits with a pretty ribbon. Then she would dress me in one of my Sunday-school dresses. Most of them had puffed up sleeves, gathered waists, and ribbons which tied at the back and, of course, my white shoes, with white ankle socks. The attire would be completed with a small straw hat, and a tiny bag with straps, which I would sling over my shoulder.

In my little bag, Mother would put some crackers (biscuits), some sweets, a handkerchief and my collection (offering). This would be about one penny. Some of the children used their offering to buy sweets! I never did that because Mother told me that if I did God would punish me. Sunday-school was about two miles from where I lived, and I walked to and from Sunday after Sunday, and thought nothing of it! In those days there was no public transport that ran on Sundays, or most days, therefore, children and adults had no choice, they had to walk. Looking back now at the distance as I see it in my mind, made me wonder how on God's earth did I do it! Yet in those days it was the normal thing to do. My favourite Sunday-school songs were:

(1) Jesus wants me for a sunbeam,

After Sunday school I would stay on to join in the adult worship, as Mother would be attending. If the Captain (this was what they called the Salvation Army Minister), was not able to attend for any reason, my mother would conduct the service. I loved the adult worship. They had a complete band of musical instruments. My favourite was the clarinet and the drums. The church was a very large building. Comparing to today's standard I would say, it was like any modern church. There were wooden pews on either sides of the aisle and a very large congregation. In those days most people went to church. The Salvation Army attracted people from a number of districts, mainly because of the music and my mother, who was a very good singer and preacher. After service, Mother sometimes stopped for refreshment at one of the member's house, who lived next door to the church. This was very welcome, because after a very lengthy service I was very hungry, and thirsty.

On the way home from church sometimes, if we were lucky, we would see the occasional car going in our direction, the driver would offer us a lift. My mother, sister and brother would be overjoyed at the offer, but I was not very eager to accept! I wanted to walk, so that I could hear the noise made by my shoes as I walked on the stones on the road! Reluctantly I had to accept the lift, my mother insisted.

Apart from dressing up on Sundays, and wearing my white shoes, there was another incentive. My father's egg punch! My father could not make himself a cup of coffee to save his life, although he was a strong coffee drinker. He believed that cooking was a woman's perogative, but he loved making egg-punch. He thought noone could make egg-punch better than himself. Every Sunday morning, before breakfast, he would call one of the children to bring him this large mixing bowl and a wooden spoon. He then got some eggs, bottles of stout, white rum, cow's milk, sweet condensed milk, nutmeg, vanilla and a little sugar (wet sugar). I will talk about this kind of sugar later on. He would mix these ingredients together for quite some time until the contents became light and frothy. Then out came the

glasses, one for each of us, and one for mother. The amount
we got varied according to age, Dad would have his special
silver tankard (a large mug-type container). He told me, this
was to make me grow into a strong girl! Mother always left
hers until she returned from church. Sometimes she would
return to find the glass empty. Dad would drink it for her!

Sunday dinners were a real treat. Mum always cooked
something special. My favourite was roast beef, red kidney
beans and rice, slices of yellow yams, and a side salad. This
would be followed by soursap juice (a fruit), or freshly made
carrot juice. Then there was the bonus of clearing Dad's
table. My dad always left some of his dinner and drink for
me on a Sunday! In those days this was a treat for small
children. My older brother and sister were quite jealous of
this, as Sunday dinners were special. There was no shortage
of food for the family, leaving some of Dad's food for the
children was a tradition. Dad ate hot pepper with all his
meals (country pepper). He planted one pepper tree right
outside the kitchen window. At meal times he would pick
a really ripe juicy one, washed it and just bit it as he ate
his meals, seeds included! Sometimes he would cut the
pepper into small slices and add to the food. If you did not
know that the pepper was added and you just bit into the
rice and peas, or the roast beef, no amount of water could
stop the burning. I gradually got use to eating hot pepper.
I suppose that is the reason why, until this day, I eat hot
pepper with almost everything. I am the only one in the
family who likes hot pepper. Thanks to Dad. At week days,
Dad would use a rota system of table clearing. It was as if
he had a photographic memory. If I tried to cheat when it
was not my turn to clear the table, Dad would say, "It's not

your turn, you cleared the table Tuesday," or something of that nature. He would remember exactly whose turn it was without keeping a diary. We used to use the leftover (as we called it) as bargaining chips. If Mother asked one of us to go to the shop for instance, we would say to someone else, "If you go to the shop for me, you can clear dad's table." First, we would have to tell Dad of the agreement!

Nursery school was not available in my childhood days, but (private) nursery schools for the under-sevens were, for the parents who could afford to pay. One of these schools was located in the adjoining district from where I lived, approximately one and a half miles away. This school was run by a retired teacher, who was also the Registrar of Births and Deaths. It was so much in demand; I was told that parents often put their children's names on the waiting list when they registered their births! Unfortunately, not all parents could do this because of financial difficulties; they could not afford the weekly fees. There was no help from the government, therefore, only the privileged whose parents could afford to pay the fees, had this very important basic education. I was one of the lucky ones who attended private school as they were called. My beloved mother, who had to make great sacrifices, made sure I did. (God bless her spirit.)

Secondary and junior schools were incorporated in the same building, and the hours were the same: 9 a.m. sharp and finished at 4.30 p.m. This was very convenient for my mother because my elder sister and brother had to pass the nursery school on their way to secondary school. The nursery school was at the junction on the right, and the secondary school was on the left, approximately half a mile up a slight hill. They would drop me off on their way to school, and collected me on their way home. Thus saving my dear mother having to walk one and a half miles in the morning and another one and a half miles in the evening, to take and collect me from school.

I remember very clearly the events leading up to me commencing secondary/junior school. My beloved mother bought the material (navy and white) for my school uniform. I wore a navy pleated skirt and white blouse, black shoes and white socks. The uniform for the older children who were in the higher grades was the same. Mother gave the materials to my godmother who was living very near to me, to be made up. I remember collecting my uniform when it was completed. I took it home and mother pressed it and hung it on a hanger in her room, under what was called "the hanging shelf". This was a shelf with hooks underneath, and covered around with curtains. Very few people had proper wooden wardrobes. These were found mainly in rich people's homes. I kept going into the room to admire my new school uniform!

When the big day finally arrived I was very nervous. Mother woke very early, around 6 o'clock, cooked breakfast, packed my lunch box, made some drinks, usually sweetened cow's milk or diluted condensed milk, or "lemonade" which was water sweetened with sugar and lime juice, was then added. Lunch usually consisted of fried dumplings with fried eggs or hard dough bread and butter, with cheese. Fruits were not included as these were in abundance everywhere. Children normally just helped themselves to anybody's fruit trees. Mother took me to school herself. Made sure I was settled, gave me a hug, and left! I cried for a while, then I tried to get used to being among a whole class of strange children, and a strange teacher.

I was put in A Class, which was the beginners' class in the junior section (first year). Then B Class (second year). Then third Class (third year). One moved up the grading ladder until the final school year.

There was a system in which senior students could have private after-school lessons. These lasted over a period of three years. These lessons were quite expensive, therefore, accessibility could only be accessed to students whose parents could afford to pay. Some students could only afford to stay on for the first year, others for two years, while others could afford to complete the full three years. At the end of each year, students had to sit an examination. If they were successful they would be awarded a certificate. If they failed the exam they were allowed to re-sit. Of course, those who were fortunate to be able to afford to stay on for three years, and were successful in all the examinations, would be awarded the Third Year Certificate of Higher Education. This is a very prestigious certificate, equivalent to the U.K. GCE (General Certificate of Education).

This certificate would help students to enter high school. After completing high school, they could then go on to collages or university.

Attending private nursery school was to my advantage because when I started junior school, I already had basic education which started in the first year (A class). Because of this, I was not kept in A class. I was moved to B class and also proved too advanced for this class. I was then moved to First class, where, after a short time, was moved to Second class, where I finally settled.

School discipline in the 1930s was so strict, it was almost cruel. Some teachers were almost like cruel task masters!

They were very strict on time keeping. School commenced at 9 a.m. sharp, and if you were five minutes late, you would get the cane! Girls were beaten in the palms of their hands, and boys would have their trousers pulled down and beaten on their buttocks, bent over a chair in front of the entire class, which was mixed. I had the cane on several occasions for being late. I can still feel the burning in the palms of my hands, as I bring this cruel punishment to memory. The boys had great welts on their buttocks for days. My brother showed me his! There was this particular male teacher who, I think, got great satisfaction from caning children. He was quite a big man and looked very fearsome. The female teachers used to send the children from their classes to this 'monster' to be caned. He was about 5ft 10ins tall, of light complexion and had wavy hair, which he always parted in the middle.

After assembly there was the daily inspection of finger nails. The children were made to line up, and the teacher of that individual class would shout, "Stretch out your hands." She/he would then inspect each child's fingernails. If the nails were not spotlessly clean, you would get the cane. After the examination of fingernails, came the examination of hair, uniform and shoes! Needless to say if your hair was not neatly combed, uniforms not clean and well pressed, and shoes wellpolished (those whose parents could afford shoes), you would first get a telling off, followed by the cane. This time the boys would be lucky, they would be beaten in the palms of their hands, same as the girls. If your uniform was unsatisfactory on more than one occasion, a letter would be sent to your parents. If this was not rectified, you would be expelled.

To keep my fingernails clean, I used a shrub-like plant which looked like sugar cane. It had joints, the same as sugar cane, quite soft and juicy, and grew by the sides of the roads, which was very convenient because as I ran along the road, if my nails were not spotlessly clean, I would just break some lizard cane, as this cane-like shrub was called, and as I ran along with my school bag over my shoulder, I would be cleaning my nails at the same time!

Children got the cane, or beating as it was called, for things such as talking in class, looking at other people's work, copy taking as this was called, not getting your arithmetic right, not reading well, not finishing your homework, eating sweets during lessons, not paying attention to the teacher, the list is endless! You got more beatings at school than you had at home! Some parents came to the school and cursed the teachers for beating their children. Some parents became quite violent and help had to be summoned from other classes. Some teachers got punched. The highlight of the day for us as small children was when we saw an angry father approaching the school, especially if they were coming to see "the monster" as we called the headteacher!

Some parents moved their children to another school which was in the adjoining district because of the beatings of their children by the headmaster. This was such a shame because this school was in a very pleasant area, slightly up hill, with large play areas, a stand pipe, and lots of fruit trees. The church was also on the same plot of land, a few chains from the school. It was very huge, situated on top of the hill, and could be seen miles away. It had a very huge pipe organ which, when played, could be heard from my home which was approximately one and a half to two miles away.

The bell could also be heard from my home, and acted as a community clock. Every morning the bell would ring at 8 a.m. and again at about 8:45am. 'First bell' as we used to say, acted as a warning that it was time to leave for school, and 'second bell' warned that you had only quarter of an hour. My mother was very concerned about us getting the cane for being late. She would shout, "Hurry up, first bell is gone." There were several churches about, but people felt quite proud to be a member of this 'unique' church. The minister was a white man. He was well loved by everyone, children and adults.

Half a pint of cow's milk was given to the children daily, free school milk as it was called. Children had to bring their own containers to receive this milk. Regarding school lunch, there were three choices: packed lunch, money to buy whatever you fancied for school lunch, or have school dinners. The British currency was in use, as the island had not yet had independence. Many children preferred the second choice because they would get at least two-pence for lunch. From this they would buy one Bulla cake (a large flat sweet cake). That left them with one penny, which they would spend on sweets. Mainly mint-balls, paradise plums, or strongback (types of sweets). They would save their free school milk and drink it at lunchtime with the Bulla cake. The currency was one pound (paper), ten shillings (paper), five shillings (paper) half a crown, or two and six (silver) two shillings, one shilling, sixpence (which was half of a shilling) three pence (which was half of sixpence) then two pence, one penny, half-penny and a farthing (which was a very small silver coin). Things were very, very cheap, so for two pence, if you were clever, you could buy your lunch and have money left over! School dinners were very nice. Each day of the week, the cooks would prepare something different. There was curry goat and plain rice, beef soup with ground food added such as yams, Irish potatoes, dumplings and pumpkins. Some days we would have red kidney beans and rice with a choice of meat. There were no free school dinners, so the children whose parents could not afford to pay, were provided with a separate menu! This was almost mainly cornmeal porridge and hard dough bread and butter. Some of the dinner ladies were very nice, and sometimes gave proper dinners to the poorer children who couldn't afford to pay, although if the head caught them, they would get into trouble. The "poor class" dinner, as other children called the dinners for the poorer children, was very cheap.

One could change from one option to another. I liked curry goat and rice, so on the day when that was on the menu, I would have school dinner. There was a small room set aside, which had shelves; this was used to keep children's pack lunch boxes. The door was shut but not locked. Every day somebody's lunch would be stolen. The unfortunate child would dash into the cloakroom, as it was called, and would burst out crying. Their lunch box was found to be empty! Someone would creep into the cloakroom, perhaps when they went to the toilet, and ate other children's lunch. That child would be sent home at lunch time because they had nothing to eat. This happened so often that children began to watch who went to toilet often during lessons. There was this particular girl who was from a very poor family, who kept going to the toilet. She was observed for days, and then the teacher decided to check the "cloakroom" one day after she went to the toilet and stayed a long time. She was caught red-handed eating someone's lunch! Apart from being humiliated before the entire class, she got the cane. From that day children called her "lunch thief". Children can be very cruel. Looking back now I felt sorry for the girl. I am not saying that she was entitled to steal other children's lunches, but she had a good reason to do so. Her parents could not afford to give her packed lunches, or dinner money, or even "poor class" school dinner money. She always went home at lunch times for her "lunch." She lived very near the school, about ten minutes' walk.

My favourite games at play times, as we called break times, were skipping, baseball, playing cricket with the boys, running and hide and seek. When playing hide and seek, I used to go under the school. The building was slightly raised on blocks, therefore if you bend very low or crawl on your hands you could go right under. I also liked high jump, although I was not very good at this. Break times were a real treat as it was always very hot in the school. It was lovely to be out in the open air, there was always a breeze blowing which kept you feeling cool. Sometimes if I didn't feel like playing I used to just sit under a very large Poinciana tree. This was a tree which had branches that covered a very large area, thus acted as shade from the sun. "Shady tree" it was called. It also blossomed into red petals, which, when in bloom, looked really beautiful.

At four-thirty the closing hymn was, "The day Thou gavest, Lord is ended, The darkness falls at Thy behest, To Thee our morning hymns ascended, Thy praise shall sanctify our rest. Amen." I loved that song. Not only that it was a good feeling to have come to the end of what was sometimes a very hard day, but my class had some very good singers, and the voices just belted out the tune.

Unfortunately, I was moved from that school to another school as did most children because of the headmaster. There was a continuous barrage of arguments between parents and the head, caused because of his love of the cane. My older sister and brother were also moved to this other school. This school was in my district, and the distance was approximately the same as the school that I was moved from. To get to my first school, I turned right at the bottom of my road, to get to this present "new" school I turned left. This school was not far from the Salvation Army where I attended Sunday school.

The school was on a large plot of land, very close to the main road. The school ground, and the grounds of the teacher's cottage, was just like an orchard. There was almost every kind of fruit tree crammed together. Oranges, mangoes, tangerine (flat orange-type fruit), mandarin (as tangerine but bigger), star apples, apples, plums, breadfruit, the list was endless. Although I did not get verbal approval from the headmaster, myself and other children picked and ate fruits at break time and after school, to our hearts desire! The teacher's cottage (bungalow) was on the same plot of land. It was situated a few chains below the school, to the left at the end of a very pleasant grass patch of land. It was a large building, very spacious with a veranda on which laid comfortable veranda chairs. The headmaster had a maid, and a small secondhand car, which was counted a luxury in those days, as only very few people owned motor cars. He was not married, and had no family.

This headmaster was an angel compared to the previous headmaster. He was a real gentleman. Very quietly spoken, and I honestly can't remember him losing his cool, or using the cane! He was a very goodlooking man; tall, of smooth dark complexion, with a small mouth and a straight nose. He had good quality hair as though he was mixed with Indian. He always parted his hair to the side. He had a lovely smile, which made him even more handsome. The older girls all had a crush on him.

There was another good quality to this headmaster. He would never pass anyone on the roads in his little car without stopping and offering them a lift. He was liked by children and parents alike.

On joining the school, I continued in the class that I was in at the school that I left. The routine was the same, strict timekeeping, neat and tidy appearance, well-groomed hair, and clean finger-nails. This was standard practice. If one was late they would not get the cane, but during roll call if you were not in school when the register was called, you would be recorded absent. If this happened too often a letter would be sent to your parents. The parents would then give you a beating, because the teacher would blame the parents for not seeing to it that the child got to school on time!

Instead of frequent use of the cane, detention was used as punishment. The teacher would use chalk to draw a big circle, usually on the platform. The circle would be made before school closed and left as a deterrent. After school was closed the child would then stand in the middle of the circle for one hour. After completing detention, there was the long walk home, which meant getting home quite late. On arriving home, hungry and tired, after running and walking fast to complete the long journey before dusk, there was the fear of getting a beating from your parents. Once home you had to explain the reason for detention, and would almost certainly get a beating, which meant that you were no better off not getting the cane from the teacher in the first place!

My favourite subjects at school were Scripture (Religious Studies), English and Science. I hated maths. Maths was my worst subject. Because of my dislike for this subject, I made little or no effort to learn. I depended on my friend who sat next to me. She was a walking computer. She would finish her maths in minutes, and then she would slip her finished work to me and did my work. During the time that she was doing my work I pretended to be writing. She would complete my maths work and slip me the exercise book (maths book) again with all the correct answers, the same as hers. One day my luck ran out, and I was caught by the teacher. She was very tactful in the way that she handled the situation. I knew that she had noticed that I had my friend's maths book, and that I was pretending to be writing, because she paused for a long time to look at my work, before she moved on. My heart started to race because I knew then that I was going to be punished. She calmly collected the books, marked everyone's work, handed back the maths books, commented on how brilliant we all were, then she cleaned the blackboard and stood on the platform beside the clean blackboard with a piece of white chalk in her hand. She then looked at the class, turning her head from side to side, as though she was not planning on calling anyone in particular. She then pointed to me and said, "Gloria, can you come and show the class how you arrived at your answers." I felt numb. I could hardly get up from my seat. I eventually pulled myself up from my seat and swallowed hard, as I suddenly developed a lump in my throat. I walked up to the blackboard, took the piece of chalk from the teacher's hand and started to cry. Needless to say I could not do the maths. I could not remember experiencing embarrassment like that during my entire school life!

Apart from getting the 'circle treatment' which was standing in the middle of a large white circle made with white chalk for one hour after school (detention), I was told to write the words 'copy taker' in capital letters one hundred times. 'Copy taker' was the term used when you copied work or asked someone else to do the work. From that day until today, I never forgot that experience. It is still very clear in my mind. That public humiliation made me try harder at maths. I was still not good at the subject but I never asked anyone to do my work again!

Recalling my school days, I would honestly say, apart from maths, I was quite a bright student. This incident happened when I was age 9 or 10. Looking back to those days now I laugh because I now see the funny side of the incident, but at the time when it happened, I did not think that it was funny. As a matter of fact I was very embarrassed. Not only on that day, but for a long time because I was teased and laughed at by other children for quite some time. The school inspector was visiting my school. This was standard practice. School inspectors would visit periodically to check the standard of teaching, and generally to see first-hand how the children were getting on. On this particular day, the inspector was visiting my class. He sat on a desk, face towards the class. Looking back now at the incident I understand why he did not sit on a chair. He wanted to make the children feel comfortable. Children were terrified of school inspectors. The reason was because the inspectors would ask questions, make us read, do maths etc. Children would be quite nervous when we were told that the Inspector would be visiting. Some inspectors could be quite harsh, even more so than the teachers.

They would walk in, dressed in a suit and tie, carrying a briefcase. That was enough to make the children nervous. They were quite serious, seldom smiled (except for the nice ones). The one who visited my class this day in question was very nice. He sat on the desk, smiled and said, "Who can recite 'My Strength'?" I put my hand up; I was the only one to do so. The inspector looked at me, smiled and said, "You can recite 'My Strength'?"

"Yes Sir" I said I stood up, hands to my side (stood to attention) and shouted out, "My strength!" and sat down. Well the inspector roared out laughing, so did all the class. I thought he was just testing our English. After he managed to stop laughing, he explained that my strength was the first two words of a recitation called 'My Strength'. From that day I was called "My Strength". That name stuck to me for a very long time!

One of my best friends at that school was a girl who came from a very poor family. She had an older sister and a brother. All three attended the same school. Their mother died, and they were brought up single-handed by their father. All three children attended school barefoot (without shoes). The two sisters had only one school uniform. It got washed so often that the colour of the navy blue skirt faded to almost white! Their blouses were often patched. The boy's khaki uniform was also patched. The youngest girl, who was one of my best friends, was a very bright student. She came first in all subjects! I am not ashamed to say she was brighter than me. Because of their social status, they were very isolated. Most children refused to mix with them, especially at break times. My friend completed secondary education, and then went on to teacher's college. The last I heard of her, she was teaching! The older sister also did fairly well and the last I heard of her, she was the manager in a top peoples' store. The brother left school and joined the Army.

Another incident which stuck in my mind happened one day as reading class was in progress outside under a large shady mango tree. Classes were often held outside as the heat was sometimes unbearable in the school rooms. I looked and saw a teacher frogmarching a girl towards my class. The girl was a sixth-former. Her teacher said sorry for interrupting the reading class. She then pointed to me and asked me to, "Teach this girl to spell 'bed'." I was very sorry for the girl, because she was so embarrassed. My complete class was shocked. After I spelt "bed", the teacher made her write "bed" one hundred times on the blackboard. Not only was she humiliated, but she was nick-named "bed". She was involved in several fights because of this name calling.

There was one day of the year called Empire Day. This was to remind us that we were part of the British Empire. On this unique day all schools were given a holiday from school. Schools from several districts would meet at their individual schools at 9 o'clock in the morning in their school uniforms. Then they would march with the British flag, red, white and blue, held high and singing, "Rule Britannia!" They marched to this particular school which had a large plot of grass land, just like a lawn, a short distance from this school. Some schools marched for a distance of three miles to congregate at this playing field. They would then compete against each other at all kinds of games. At the end of the day a trophy would be rewarded to the winning school. The winning school would then keep the trophy for one year, to be competed for the following year.

I used to look forward to Empire Day. Apart from taking part in different kinds of sport, there was the maypole. I loved dancing under the maypole. I had a great laugh when other children got their ribbons knotted up! Then there was music, and women selling all kinds of delicacies, cakes, sweets, ice creams, and many more. This was the one day of the year when children got extra pocket money for lunch. I got two shillings from my dear mother; father would give me another shilling, making a grand total of three shillings. For the rest of the year, the losing schools would practice very hard at games to try and win the trophy the following year. One of the incentives of Empire Day was the opportunity of mixing with children from different schools. At the end of the day I would have quite a bit of my spending money left over. So did most children. This money would be put into my savings box to top up my 'Christmas money'.

I had a very strict upbringing. My father was a very strong disciplinarian. He spent most of his life living in Cuba, spoke fluent Spanish, and served in the 1914 war. I, along with my older brother and sister, would get a beating from my father for what seemed unnecessary incidents. He was very strict about the time we got home from school. If my sister and I were not home from school by his deadline, we would arrive home to find my father standing on the veranda with his cow's skin whip in his hands (plaitted strands of dried cow's skin)! There was nothing that we could tell him to prevent him beating us. Although he did not say

it in so many words, I think that he thought that if we were
late home, it meant that we were fooling around with boys,
as this was a mixed school. My dear mother would get quite
upset when Dad beat us. He used to tell her, "I will not save
the rod and spoil the child."

My older brother used my father's home from school
deadline to his advantage! If I had a disagreement with
my brother, and he wanted my father to beat me without
actually telling him to, he would make sure that he got home
from school before I did. He had an old bicycle wheel, he
then used a piece of wire, (like a coat hanger), only longer.
He bent one end of the wire to form a hook which he then
slid under the bicycle wheel and pushed the wheel along.
This made the wheel run along at extraordinary speed.
He called this his car. As soon as school is dismissed, my
brother would be out like a flash, and off he went running
behind his "car" at great speed. There was no way that I
could keep up with him for a distance of over one and a
half miles! It meant that he would get home from school
long before me. I would then arrive home exhausted,
trying to keep up with my brother's running, only to find
my father standing on the veranda with his cow's skin whip
in his hands. He would shout his usual question, "where
have you been? How comes your brother gets home before
you?" Before I had the chance to answer I would get several
lashes with the whip!

Apart from the cow's skin whip, my father used a thing
called 'suble jack'. This is a flexible cane which was cut and
dried in the sun. Something like the cane that the teachers
used. If he wanted to give a 'medium' beating he would use
the 'suble jack'. If he was really angry and wanted to give a

'good beating' as he called it, he would use the cow's skin whip!

No child was allowed to call an adult by their first name. It was always Mrs, Miss, Mr or Mass, which means Mr. Children were not allowed to nod or shake their head when spoken to by an adult. It was always, "Yes, sir," or "Yes, mam." "No, sir," or "No, mam." If one dared to answer otherwise you would get the sharp reaction of, "Who do you think you are talking to? You think you and I are company?" If you nod or shake the head the reaction would be very sharp: "Don't nod or shake your head while I am speaking to you." If you were lucky, often you would get a slap, accompanied by the reminder, "You have a mouth, use it." Discipline was the order of the day.

Everybody knew everybody, both in one's own district, and in other districts. Therefore, if a child was caught on the roads misbehaving by any adult, that adult had the right to slap that child and give him or her a good telling off! The child could not go home and complain to their parents because their parents would want to know the reason why they had a slap from that particular adult. If the child did complain to their parents and it was proven that they were misbehaving, the parents of that child would give the child a beating! Therefore, if a child was rude and got a slap from an adult, they would keep quiet about it for fear of getting a beating from their parents.

When passing someone's house, be it a neighbour or someone three miles away, as long as you knew the name of the person who lived in that house, you would not go by without saying, "Good morning," or "Good evening." Even if you don't see the person, but if you suspect that they are at home, you would shout out a loud, "Good morning, Miss Esther," or, "Good evening, Mass Joel." If the person did not answer first time, you would shout louder a second time to make sure that the person heard you. This was done by adults and children alike. The reason is that it was counted bad manners to go past somebody's house without 'calling to them'. If you did go by without 'calling' to the person, and the person found out later that you went past their house without 'calling to them', they would not be very pleased. If they found out that you went past their house even days or weeks later without 'calling to them', and they saw you after that, they would say, "You went past my house last Friday and did not even call to me, what have I done to you?"

There were no police or police stations for miles. There was no need for them. Discipline was instilled in children from a very young age, and was followed up in schools. Therefore, crime was almost non-existent. People would leave their homes unlocked, with noone at home for the whole day, and returned to find everything intact.

I first saw a policeman and a police station when I was a teenager and went to live in the town. When I arrived in the town I was very surprised to see so many cars! One day I was walking along this particular street when I saw this beautiful car parked by the side of this street. I stopped to admire the car and then made a very big mistake of proceeding to touch this car! Suddenly a man dashed from inside a shop across the street, and gave me one almighty slap across my face, my head almost fell off. He then swore at me and told me, never to touch his car again. I went off holding my face in my hands, the pain was intense. On my arrival home, I could not tell anyone because I would only be told off for touching the man's car. Perhaps I would get a beating as well as a telling off!

As children we all had our household chores to perform. Some chores had to be done before we went to school. Others were done when we returned from school, and some were done on Saturdays. Most of my older brothers and sisters had left home and gone to live in the towns. Remaining at home were two older brothers, one brother and one sister still at school, and myself, also my nephew, who had been brought up by mother. My two older brothers were given the task of helping my father with farming the land, and generally were put in charge of looking after the cows, mules, horses, donkeys, pigs and goats. Apart from farming, my father had lots of animals. There were also lots of chickens. I loved feeding the chickens. I would stand in the middle of the yard with a container of dried sweetcorn grains in a container, and called out quite loud, "Chick, chick, chick, come, come, come," and before long the chickens would try to get in on the act, but I would drive them away! I would have one or more chickens for myself, given to me by my father. He always made sure that he gave us either chickens or goats or sometimes, a pig for ourselves. The boys usually got goats or pigs. Sometimes they would be given chickens as well. I usually made sure that my chicken or chickens were well fed! Sometimes they got overfed and became so fat that they could not lay eggs and had to be eaten! My older brother loved it when I overfed my chickens. I thought that I was being clever feeding my chickens more often than the other chickens. There was no shortage of eggs. Nests, as they were called was made by nailing kerosene oil tins, cut in half, or any kind of tins large enough for the chickens

to sit comfortably in. These were then lined with dried
banana leaf or dried grass, and nailed in rows to the back
of the wooden kitchen. Apart from leaving some of the eggs
to hatch, father usually sold some. Eggs were sold by the
dozen. Traders, mainly women from other districts, would
call at certain days to buy eggs. They carried large baskets on
their heads, and would shout, "Eggs, any eggs?"

One of the duties which had to be performed before
going to school was, to make sure that there was an adequate
supply of drinking water, and water for general household
use. The water was stored in two large barrels, one for
drinking and one for general household use, such as washing
of dishes and clothes, bathing etc. Collecting water was the
duty of my elder brother and sister who were still at school,
and me. The water was carried on our heads in kerosene
tins, buckets, or any clean vessel which was suitable for this
purpose. Water for household purpose was not a problem as
this was taken from two ponds (large waterholes), both quite
near to where I lived. One pond was owned by a wealthy
neighbour, and the other was owned by a very rich white
man, who owned acres of land. Drinking water also came
from his property. This was stored in a tank; a kind of very
deep circular swimming pool, which was covered over with
zine and mesh wire to prevent debris such as leaves falling
into the water. This "tank" also served people from adjoining
districts with drinking water. Although the owner of this
tank did not give verbal consent for people to take drinking
water from his tank, he did not really mind. He was quite
aware that water was being taken because the quantity of
water in the tank would decrease rapidly during dry season.
If the water level got too low he would become concerned

that there would not be enough water for his use, and would get the ranger to keep watch!

When this happened, it meant that we had to get up very early, around 4 o'clock in the morning to walk about four miles, two miles each way, to collect drinking water from a special pond (water hole), owned by another wealthy landowner. It would be quite dark when we set out on our journeys. Therefore, we carried torches as there were no electric lights! The torches were made by my older brother. This was made by putting kerosene oil in empty bottles and inserting a wick which was made with a piece of old clothing. We would walk very fast so that we could get to the pond before the wick burnt out! By the time we collected the water and were half way home, it would be light enough for us to see without the use of the torch. Because of the distance, we could only make one trip before going to school.

Poorer families, who could not afford suitable vessels for carrying water, used goards (a very large fruit-like object), something like an oversized grapefruit. This was not edible. It was used as a vessel for carrying or storing water. The inside would be scraped out after making a circular cut-out at the top. Some people would split the goards in half before they got two large, scrape out the inside, and use it as a drinking vessel. If children knew of a family who used goards, they would nickname them "goardie"!

During our early morning water carrying session, we would arrange to meet other children who were also carrying water at the same time. I quite enjoyed the company as we would have a chat and a laugh.

When we came home from school the water carrying would start all over again, as the water which was collected for household purposes would be used up during the day! I hated the after school water carrying because after a somewhat hard day at school, and walking approximately three miles home, one doesn't feel very energetic. To avoid having to make several trips, I would fill the container to the brim. When this happens, the water would splash over the edge of the container, and by the time I got home, I would be soaked! The other mishap was, sometimes I would be a short distance from home with my precious container of water, and would slip, losing the lot! This meant double trouble, spilling the water, getting soaked to the skin, and having to go all the way back to the pond to collect the water! Apart from all these problems, sometimes when I got home, wet and tired, my father would tell me off for spilling the water and getting wet! When this happens it meant two trips to the pond, but actually taking home only one container of water. By the time I got home, it would be time for dinner. After dinner, it was homework time. This meant that I had not carried enough water for the evening and would have to make the extra trip the following evening! Other times I did not need to, as mother, who was always very sympathetic, would try to cut down on the use of water for that day, so that the barrel would still be half full. That meant that I would only have to make one or two trips after school. Water for household use was a daily routine. Sometimes we would make one trip before school and several trips after school. Drinking water was fetched once or twice per week, depending on how thirsty the family was! Drinking water was very precious and was stored with great care. The barrels were kept covered, and anyone who forgot to replace the cover after taking water from the drinking-water barrel, as it was called, would be severely told off by my parents, or even by the other children. Sometimes traders, strangers, people who had to pass my house to get to their house, children coming from school, would all call in for a drink of water. This was usual practice. One doesn't have to know the family to stop and ask for a drink of water. As a child, I noticed that some people made it a habit to always stop at our house for water to drink. Needless to say, I was not very pleased. I often said to myself, "Why do they always want water from our house?" They would go past several houses, but would always wait until they got to my house to ask for drinking water. Not that I would refuse giving anyone a drink of water, but depending on how many people stopped for drinking water, and how thirsty they are (some people would drink two and three large glassfuls). I would be thinking that the drinking water is going too fast, which, if continued at this alarming rate, would mean me having to fetch drinking water more than once or twice for the week. Apart from the distance, this meant getting out of bed at 4 o'clock more than once for that week!

Gathering firewood, cleaning the house and sweeping the yard was done on Saturdays. Firewood was needed for cooking as there was no gas or electric cookers. Even the very rich had stoves, cookers which were operated by use of coal or firewood. My family's kitchen was an outer building made of boards with a thatched roof. The cooking area was a raised built-up area like a barbeque. In the middle of the barbeque were three large stones on which were placed pieces of flat irons to form a square. The square could be adjusted to accommodate more than one pot, by adding more large stones and more pieces of iron. The pots are usually made of copper, and had three legs. Then there was the Dutch pot which was shallower, followed by the frying pan. All were made of the same very heavy material, (copper). The firewood was cut into fairly short pieces and neatly arranged under the pot or pots. Cooking with firewood was very quick (if you used the right kind of firewood). If you used a poor type of firewood, this would give off lots of smoke and, apart from becoming exhausted from continuous blowing puffs of air with your mouth or fanning with whatever is to hand that will produce a gust of air to try to keep the firewood alight, you would get watery eyes from excess smoke! At the end of cooking, which would take a very long time, the food would sometimes taste of smoke!

Good quality firewood was very important to my mother. Not only did she need good wood for cooking, but also for heating the iron for ironing clothes. This is a manual iron made from iron, shaped almost like the electric iron of today, but smaller and without the dials but, of course, it had a handle. There was also another type of iron which was mostly used by tailors, called a tailor iron. This was much heavier. It was opened up and lighted coal was put inside. It was then closed and ready for use. Both types of iron were very effective, and did a good job of ironing the clothes. Of course, in those days, one was counted very fortunate if they were the proud owner of a tailor iron. To heat the smaller iron, which was also quite heavy, Mother would lay a fairly thick length of firewood, to form what she called "the backing". Then pieces of smaller firewood, all lengthways, then she would put three of four irons in a row close to the firewood and each other. The irons would become hot in a very short time. She would then take the irons alternately clean the face of the iron without touching the now very hot iron, by means of rubbing the "face" of the iron on a piece of damp cloth which she kept on the "ironing board". She ironed on a table. Everybody called the table-top the "ironing board". I first saw a real ironing board when I went to live in the town. The very top-quality firewood was got from a tree called logwood. These trees were mostly to be found on the property of a very rich white landowner. Apart from the ranger, who carried a double-barrel shotgun, there was the added danger of being mauled by very fearsome bulls. Because of these two dangerous factors, firewood was the responsibility of my two older brothers who had finished school but were still at home. My big brothers knew exactly where these "special" logwood trees were on this property, although this property was very large. Hundreds of acres. Regardless of the dangers my young sister, brother and I went along with my big brothers on a Saturday to collect firewood, although I did not tell them my reason for tagging along. I went because of the mangoes! There were all kinds of mangoes on this property. I loved mangoes! While my brothers were busy cutting up the firewood into suitable lengths, I was busy eating mangoes. There were also lots of other fruits on the plantation, oranges, star apples, and grapefruits, to name but a few. People came from adjoining districts to get firewood and to eat fruits. This was done at your own risk. We were never caught, neither were any of my friends. The firewood was then tied up in bundles and carried on the head home.

After returning home from the firewood gathering, it was time to sweep the yard. The house (bungalow) in which I lived stood on approximately four to six acres of land. The yard was very big. There was a large lawn to the front of the house, on the right. Then there was another large area at the back of the house, which carried on along the side past the kitchen, and on to the left for quite a distance, then back towards the border of my nearest neighbour, and along the front of the veranda. Apart from the size of the yard, there were lots of fruit trees nearby, and if it was windy the wind would blow the leaves all over the yard. This was not an easy task. The sweeping of the yard was the responsibility of my older brother, sister and me. We usually divided the yard into three areas. That way each would do their fair share of sweeping.

When the sweeping of the yard was completed, it was time to clean the house and the outside toilet. Cleaning the house included polishing and shining the floors. Again this was the responsibility of the three of us. I would polish and shine the veranda, my sister would polish and shine two bedrooms, and my brother would shine the living/dining room. I would also polish and shine the floors of the outside toilet. There was no carpet or lino. The floorboards were first swept to remove the dust, then wiped with a damp cloth, the redoak (a kind of red dye), was applied and left to dry; then beeswax, which was in hard block form, was added to the coconut brush (dried coconut sawed in two and the flesh removed). This was now a circular brush. I now kneeled on my hands and knees and pushed the well-waxed brush in a forward, backward movement along the floorboards. This resulted in a brilliant shine! The doormat was dusted and replaced. I would now stand up and back to admire my polished, well shiny floor! I would then compare my shine with my sister and brother's shine! All were of equal standard, because we used the same equipment. Then I would go off to give the same treatment to the outside toilet. My father was very particular about the cleanliness of the toilet. Perhaps it was because when he went to the toilet he seemed to spend hours smoking his cigars! If you wanted to use the toilet, and my father was "in resident", you had better make sure that you could control your bowels or you would be in big trouble. My dad was never in a hurry when he went to the toilet. It was as though he was in his bedroom!

Sunday evenings was my jewel in the crown. After returning from church and having dinner with the family, I had three choices of recreation: playing cricket, visiting my grandfather, or visiting my godmother. This was officially sealed with the authority of my father! I loved playing cricket. Games were played on a large field owned by a wealthy neighbour. The girls played against the boys. A school friend of mine and myself, were very good cricketers. Often we would beat the boys' team. Sometimes the boys would argue that it is not fair to have my friend and me on the same team playing against them. They often asked one of us to play on their side to make it fair play. Sometimes the adults would come out to watch us play. Other children would also come to support their favourite team. Usually there would be a lot of shouting and cheering when the girls were batting. The greater the support, the more boundaries we would hit!

My godmother was classed as upper-middle class. She lived in a fairly big house, which was well furnished, including a gramophone (antique record player). She had lots of records. As soon as I arrived and greeted her and the rest of her family, she would ask me to select out some

records to put on the gramophone. It really did not matter
what type of record she played. I was just so very happy
to listen to the music. If I was going to spend Sunday
evening with Godmother, as I called her, I would inform
her mid-week. She always told me not to have dinner at
home before I came, but that I should come at a given time
and have dinner with her and her family. She was a very
good dressmaker. Often times when I was ready to leave she
would hand me a parcel, nicely wrapped up. She never told
me what was in the parcel, but I always had a good idea, and
sure enough I was always right! The mystery parcel would
contain a beautiful new dress. If I did not get a dress, she
would ask the maid to pack a small box for me. This would
contain fruits, eggs, a bottle of cow's milk and a bottle of
guava jelly. She had lots of guava trees, and would use some
of the fruits to make jelly, which she knew I loved. During
my visiting times, she always gave me guava jelly and bread.
When I got home, the first thing that I would remove from
my box was my jar of guava jelly. I loved it. Unfortunately
so did everyone else! I would hide it in some cupboard or
wherever I thought noone would find it easily. It proved to
be a complete waste of time. My older brothers and sister
would always find it, and when they did, they would all but
finish the lot!

My other leisure time activity on a Sunday evening was
visiting my grandfather, "Grandpa" as I called him. He lived
approximately one mile away, in a large house surrounded by
sugar cane, lots of oranges, grapefruits, tangerines (flat orange-
type fruits), jackfruits and bread-fruit trees. The house nestled
among the orchard on a large plot of land, fairly close to the
main road. Grandpa was a white man, with milk-white hair

and blue eyes. As in the case with Godmother, whenever I am going to visit Grandpa I would inform him during the week. This was not a problem as I have to pass his house on my way to church and school. Grandpa always commanded me not to eat before I came to visit him. He would leave dinner for me. I loved visiting Grandpa. He was so very loving. I would sit on his knees and he would tell me all kinds of stories. A visit to Grandpa was triple happiness. He lived with my favourite uncle, and my uncle's daughter was my favourite cousin. This meant that I saw all my favourite side of the family at one visit. My grandpa was a retired Salvation Army officer. He would tell me all about his days in the "Army". After that it was time to play with my cousins. There was one sad aspect to my visit to Grandpa: my older uncle, who lived with the family, was isolated in a small one bedroom house to the back of the family house. He was completely blind and, although he was looked after by the family, I felt very sorry for him. He knew me by my voice, and as soon as I went in to his little house and greeted him, he would smile, and called me by my name! As a child I could not understand the reason why he did not share the family house. As I write about him, even now, I feel a deep pain for him. Sadly he died before I became an adult.

Mondays were also a unique day to me in my early childhood, as this was the day when my mother provided the family with fresh fish and lobsters. She would get up from bed very early, approximately 4 o'clock in the morning. Prior to her early morning call, she would arrange to meet another woman who lived fairly close by. Then the two ladies would set out on their long walk, approximately three miles, through rocky and winding roads, to get to the seaside. They would often take shortcuts through people's plantation to enable them to get to the seaside before the sun got to somewhat unbearable temperatures. The only problem with taking shortcuts is that they would get quite exhausted because most of the plantation through which they had to walk was mostly up hill. Apart from the hills they would get quite wet with the early morning dew. They would arrive at the seaside quite early, before it got too crowded, as Monday was the one day of the week when most housewives went to the seaside to buy fish and other sea foods.

After buying their very precious supply of fish and other sea foods, they would wait until late evening when the temperature had cooled before setting off for the long return journey home, arriving sometimes just before dusk. They would carry the fish and lobsters on their heads, in what were called pudding pans (a large flat basin). On my return home from school, if mother was not home from the seaside, I would get quite anxious, as there were rumours going around that robbers lived in the area through which they had to pass. I would sit on the stone wall which separated my parents' property from the property of our wealthy neighbour, and I would not move until I saw my mother coming down the main road. I would run to meet her and offer to carry the pudding pan of fish for her. Sometimes she would let me, at other times she wouldn't. She would say it was too heavy. Now, as I recall to memory those days, I wondered how on God's earth my dear beloved mother managed to carry that pudding pan of fish and lobsters on her head for approximately three miles!

Once I begged my mother to let me have the day off from school, so that I could go with her to the seaside. At first she was reluctant, but when I began to cry she gave in and said yes. I was very excited as I had never been to the seaside before. I had often wondered what the sea looked like. This was my big day! I was up at the crack of dawn, washed and dressed, had breakfast and was ready for my journey into the unknown. I walked for what seemed like one hundred miles! I kept asking my mother, "How much further do we have to go?" She was quite amused by the whole thing. She kept saying, "not too far." Then I walked another hundred miles. All the time I kept thinking about the return journey. I thought if God helped me to reach the seaside and return home, I would never ever ask to go to the seaside again. We went through this corn field, up a hill, and then down, passed through a large plantation which had lots of palm trees, then suddenly in the distance I had my very first glimpse of the sea! It was still quite foggy and the palms obscured my vision. I was so very happy to see the sea at last! We then walked another hundred miles through the plantation, then we came out onto a main road with shops and women by the side of the street selling all kinds of cakes, bread, fried fish, patties, ice creams, fruits and cold drinks. They were all out very early to select the best spot before the temperature got too hot! I crossed the road and at last there was the sea. I walked across the sand to the edge of the sea. At first I was very frightened, because the sea was very rough. The waves were quite high. I was fascinated at the sight of the boats which I could see in the distance. The fishermen were rowing the boats which looked so dangerous and vulnerable. I was afraid for their safety. The boats were riding the waves. I started to pray for the fishermen. "Dear God, please bring them safely to the shore."

I stood on the seashore spellbound and glued to the sand as I watched the fishermen fighting the waves in their small fishing boats. Eventually they reached the shore, got out from the boats, pulled them onto the sand and gave a big sigh. I don't know who was more relieved for their safe return to the shore, the fishermen or me. As soon as they hauled the boats out of the water onto the sand, a large crowd gathered around them. The crowd all wanted to pick the best and the biggest fish and lobsters. It became a real free-for-all. Everybody was pushing and shouting. I felt sorry for my dear mother. She kept getting pushed aside. She was not one for pushing and shouting, due to her Christian belief. There was plenty for everybody, so there was no need to push and shout. Mother got some fish from this boat then waited for another boat to come in. She bought fish from several boats. Finally, it was lunchtime and I was treated to cakes and cold drinks bought from the ladies who, by this time, took up refuge from the blazing temperature under the canopy of the grocery shops.

I sat around with my mother and the other woman under the trees, which grew along the beach, until it was time for the return journey. My mother and her friend walked so fast, I could hardly keep up with them. Finally I arrived home! I thought, *Thank God*. My poor feet were blistered and aching. I just cannot understand how my mother and her friend could make this journey every week. Some of the neighbours would come over to my house, and Mother would sell some of the fish. The money raised would go towards our education.

Some of the fish would be cooked for dinner, and the rest Mother would fry and keep in a cupboard in the kitchen to be used for dinner another day. Usually, Thursday, my older sister, brother and me would get out of bed in the middle of the night, crept out quietly, and go to the kitchen, which was a separate building a few yards from the house. We would eat some of the fried fish, and scatter the bones all over the kitchen floor, leave the dish half covered and quietly crept back into bed. In the morning when mother went to the kitchen she would automatically arrive at the conclusion that the cat had eaten the fish! That poor cat would be blamed for something she didn't do. This happened all the time. I never understood how my mother and father did not catch on that it was not the cat. I use to make it up to the cat by feeding her some of my dinner!

Wednesdays and Saturdays were also very special to me as a child. Those were the days that Mother went to the market. The market was approximately three miles from where I lived. Mother would go to the market riding on a donkey. My father or my older brother would pad the donkey (put on a kind of saddle) on the donkey's back, then on either side of the donkey were the "hampers" (containers made from wood and thatch) for carrying food stuff. Mother would then sit with her feet slightly in front of the hampers. A number of ladies would travel to the market by this kind of transport. Sometimes Mother would carry tins of wet sugar, made by my father, in the hampers to sell at the market. When she did this, she walked in front of the donkey, leading it by its rope. The money she made from the sale of the wet sugar went to buy meat and groceries and help towards our education. Market day was a big day in the lives of housewives. They would all meet at the market; all sold some form of produce grown or produce by the husbands.

Top of the list was yams, sweet potatoes, red kidney beans, and beans, all kinds of peas, fruits and wet sugar. The wet sugar was sold in a special part of the market called sugar market. This was sold by the quart, half of a quart, which was one pint, half of a pint, one gill and half of a gill, which was the smallest measure. I used to wait anxiously at the gate where I kept looking down to the main road for the return of my mother from the market. I would see women going by riding their donkeys, and chatting and laughing happily. When Mother appeared I would run to meet her. She would get down from the donkey to give me my usual ride up to the house. Then came my usual question to Mother, "What have you bought me?" Sometimes she would buy me materials for my school uniform, sometimes new shoes or socks, but she would always buy me something. She never forgot to buy me my favourite sweets, paradise plums, mint balls or strongbacks (coconut and sugar-based sweets). She would buy things for the other children or something for my father, but seldom bought things for herself. Mother always said, "The children come first." She was that kind of person, who didn't mind going without just as long as the children are not in need. On a few occasions I went with Mother to the market on a Saturday. I usually made sure that I went when she was not carrying sugar so that I could ride on the donkey. I loved strolling through the market, which was just bursting with all kinds of merchandise. I looked forward to lunchtime. Mother would ask me what I wanted for lunch. There was so much to choose from. Almost always I would choose to have beef patties (spiced beef) minced and cooked, then encased in pastry and baked; followed by a cold drink or shave ice with syrup.

Although I loved going to the market, I never went too often. The reason is that the market is located in a very flat area, and when it rains sometimes the area got flooded. The water level can rise very high within a very short time. Sometimes it is not possible for people to walk across after a very heavy shower of rain. People often got trapped in the area and were stranded until the government could arrange to send out canoes to ferry people across. When this happens, people usually say, "Painstown River come down." They call it a river because the whole area is covered with water, which makes it look just like a river. Many times folks who went to the market had to seek refuge from the volume of water in shops and rum bars, which is situated slightly on hilly areas, until the next day in some cases. Relatives usually got very worried if their loved ones didn't come home from the market after a heavy rain. They would wait up all night. The frustration is made even more painful because of the fact that there is no telephone. My mother was lucky; she never got caught on that side of the island when it rained very heavy. She was a very religious woman, and I do believe the saying that God looks after his own.

The art of cultivating was taught to us as children at a very early age. My father made sure of that. He would tell us to select a small plot of land anywhere on the land that our house was situated on, and plant our own little field, cultivating whatever we wanted to grow. There was always an argument between my older brother, sister and me. We all choose the same spot! We knew the most fertile areas, and we always argued because one would start to fork their lot and the others would start to fork the same lot! It usually took a telling-off or a beating from my father to settle the arguments! My favourite root crop was yams. I loved making the yam hills (digging the earth and piling it up to form a "mountain"). This was done in rows depending on how many yams I wanted to plant. I used to love watching the vines wind their way up the bamboo sticks which were pushed down into the ground beside the yam hills. After some time the yam vines and leaves would become bushy, thus making the small field look like a small forest. My second best root crop was sweet potatoes. I was continuously digging and looking to see if the potatoes were beginning to grow under the earth! I did the very same thing with my yams. I was always scratching under the yams to see if they were beginning to grow. It was very fascinating to see the young yams and sweet potatoes growing under the earth. I would feel very proud, and would run to tell my father that the yams and sweet potatoes were growing! Of course, my father would tell me not to keep digging and looking, because I would blight the crops. The only thing that I did not like about cultivating was the continuous weeding of the grass and weeds. As fast as I weeded the field the grass and weeds would grow back. I would get quite fed up, and would just neglect to weed the field for weeks. Of course, this meant that it would be twice as hard to weed when I finally decided to do so!

Although my father brought us up very strictly, my older brothers would find a way to be naughty without my father's knowledge. My older brother, who was responsible for looking after the pigs, had to cook food for the pigs. The cooking of the pigs' food was done in the evenings between 7 p.m. and 11 p.m. The reason was that he had to wait until dinner was finished cooking, as the pigs' food was mainly made up of the skins from the yams, sweet potatoes, breadfruit, and other ground foods. Other foods which were grown specially for feeding pigs' would be added. My brothers would arrange with their friends during the day, or sometimes days before, and would buy flour, coconut oil and pork. They would also dig yams, pick breadfruit, and hide everything until they made quite sure my father was asleep. My father loved going to bed early as he had to be up early to milk the cows then go to the plantation. When the "coast was clear", they would cook the stuff.

I often asked if I could wait up with them to join in the cooking, but would get a firm no! I could hear them chatting and laughing in the kitchen during their cooking times, as the kitchen was quite close to the house. I often wished that my father would wake from his sleep and catch them at it, but he never did. Once my father fell asleep they could rest assured that he would not wake until morning. I often threatened them that I would tell father, but did not, as I knew what they would do to me if I did.

There was another naughty thing my brothers did, unknown by my father. There was this wealthy landowner, who had acres of mango trees of all types. Noone was allowed to pick mangoes from his plantation. If children were caught picking mangoes from his plantation, they would be frogmarched to their parents, who would give them a good beating. My brothers, along with their friends, found a way to pick mangoes from this man's plantation without being caught. They would wait until it was raining heavily, then they would dress up in old clothing and have a field day picking the best mangoes from the plantation. They would return with crocus bags full of choice mangoes.

They would then change out of their wet clothing and eat mangoes to their hearts desire. What they could not eat they would they would dig a hole in the ground, lined the hole with dry banana leaves, put the mangoes in the hole, cover with another layer of leaves, and fill in with earth. They would then return to their hidden treasure whenever they felt the need to eat the mangoes.

They used the same "rain and old clothes technique" to cut and eat my father's choice sugar canes. My father always grew special soft, sweet sugar canes which we were not allowed to cut. These were grown specially to be sent along with special breadfruit and yams, and fruits, to the towns to my older sisters who lived in the towns. The sugar canes grew in bunches, therefore, when they cut one sugar cane from the bunch, they would cover the freshly cut sugar cane root with earth so that it was not easily noticeable.

Their cover got blown one day when I asked if I could join in. My brothers and their friends decided that I could join in but at a price. I would be the one to dress up in the old clothes and go out in the very heavy rain to cut the sugar cane. I thought it was fun, so I said I would do it! As I ran down the path towards the sugar cane field in the pouring rain, a piece of sharp dried wood penetrated the inside of my left foot and broke off in my foot. I screamed as the blood poured out of my foot. The pain was unbearable. I sat down on the now muddy path screaming with pain. My brothers had to dash out in the rain to carry me back to the kitchen, where one of them pulled the piece of broken wood out of my foot! I was in great pain and, when the rain stopped, I had to tell my mother what had happened. Of course, when my father came home from the plantation and was told what had happened the boys got a good beating. That foot took a very long time to heal, which prevented me from going to school for a lengthy period.

Then there was the time when I almost drowned in a waterhole. My father had this treasured breadfruit tree which was beside a waterhole. The breadfruit tree produced exceptionally large yellow and almost sweet fruits. This type of breadfruit was called yellow heart breadfruit and is the pride among the different types of breadfruits. Noone was allowed to pick breadfruit from this particular breadfruit tree without my father's permission. The breadfruit from this tree was picked solely for the purpose of being sent, along with other ground foods and fruits, to my older sisters who lived in the towns.

One Saturday, when my father was at the plantation and Mother was gone to the market, and the rest of the family were away, either with Father at the plantation, or gone to fetch firewood, or attending the animals, leaving only my brother and me at home, my brother decided to check out this prized breadfruit tree. He wanted to select a very good breadfruit to be added to the other foods that he was putting together for the night's cooking plan. He had to make quite sure that the breadfruit he had chosen to pick would not be easily missed by my father! My father would go to any length to make sure that his orders were adhered to, and it was common knowledge that he would count the fit breadfruits! My brother finally decided to pick this very large fit breadfruit which was almost obscured by leaves very high up the tree. He called me and pointed out the prized breadfruit that he had decided to pick, and told me to direct the clawed bamboo stick that he would use to pick the breadfruit, because it would be very difficult for him to see the breadfruit once he is up in the tree because of the leaves.

Unfortunately, for me to do this I had to stand quite near to the waterhole. When my brother had climbed almost to the top of this very tall tree, I started shouting to him where to direct his bamboo stick to enable him to snap off his prized breadfruit. He eventually got hold of the stem of this very large breadfruit and snapped it off with the bamboo stick.

Before I could move out of the way of the breadfruit it hit me on the head and I fell in the waterhole! I did not remember anything else until I woke up in bed with the most dreadful headache and with one of my mother's scarf's tied around my head. My poor brother was standing over me, and the fright in his eyes was dreadful. He tried to stand me up but I couldn't, I was dizzy and my head hurt so much it felt as though it would explode any minute! My brother then removed the three young breadfruit leaves which he had put inside the scarf and tied it around my forehead and replaced them with three fresh leaves. This was what people did when they had a headache, and it usually worked. Unfortunately, the "breadfruit leaf treatment" didn't work for my headache that day. Looking back on the incident in my mind now, I am quite sure I had concussion. In today's time of modern medicine, I would be kept in hospital for observation of the head injury.

It was now getting close to the time when my father and mother and the rest of the family would be home, and my headache was not getting any better. My poor brother started to cry. I felt very sorry for him. By this time a very large swelling had developed on my head, and the pain was almost unbearable. When my brother saw the swelling he cried even more, because he knew that he would have to tell the truth about what really happened. By this time I was quite sure that he had made up his mind to take the good beating that was coming to him from my father.

My mother came home before my father, and found me in bed with her scarf around my head, she was told the truth, the whole truth, and nothing but the truth. Mother felt very sorry for me, but she was also sympathetic to my brother, because she knew the beating that he would get when my father came home from the plantation. When my father came home, Mother tried to break the news to him as gently as she could, but that didn't stop him beating my brother.

There was one bus which passed through several districts and town centres and terminated in the capital city. This bus ran on certain days of the week, therefore, if you planned on going to town and, unfortunately, they missed the bus, they would not be able to make their journey until the next time that the bus was due to run.

I lived approximately one mile from the nearest bus stop. The bus would keep tooting its horn to alert people that it was on its way! I could hear the horn from approximately one and a half miles. The bus acted as a kind of community clock, as it was always on time. It was never known to be late. It would pass by at the same time on whatever day it was running. I can remember hearing my parents saying to my older brother, who would sometimes visit my sister in the town, "Hurry up, remember the bus is never late."

Apart from carrying passengers, the bus also acted as a courier service. It was the only means by which people could send baskets of food and parcels to their families and friends in the towns.

There was the driver and the sideman (conductor). The top of the bus was boxed around to enable the bus to carry unaccompanied baskets of food and parcels, which would be sent to folks living in the towns by their families and friends. There was a ladder which was fixed to the side of the bus. The sideman (conductor) would then climb up and down this ladder to pack on the top of the bus the different articles which people would ask to be taken to town.

I can remember my father packing large baskets with yams, dasheen (a kind of ground food), cassava, sweet potatoes, breadfruit, all kinds of beans and peas, sugar cane, bananas, paw paw (papaya), and all kinds of fruits to be given to the conductor of the bus to take to town for my older sister who lived in the town.

I loved following my older brother who would carry this precious basket of goodies, lovingly packed by my father's hands to be given to the conductor to take to town. He would wait until he heard the bus tooting its horn, this would be approximately one and a half miles or more away. He would take a short cut through the property of this wealthy white landowner, and he would get to the bus stop before the bus got there! The bus would make several stops to both pick up passengers, and to collect baskets and other items which would then be stored on top of the bus. Sometimes the items which were packed on top of the bus were piled up so high I could not understand how some of the things did not fall off!

I was approximately ten or eleven years old and was a very good reader. I loved English. I always pronounced my words well. On this particular day my brother was given the task of carrying this basket to the bus stop to be taken to town by the conductor of the bus. He heard the bus tooting its horn as usual, and he took his usual short cut through the property of the wealthy white landowner. We got to the bus stop at what we thought was the usual time, but as a matter of fact, the bus had already gone. Obviously the bus had fewer passengers to pick up and less baskets to collect this particular morning. Back to my "perfect English". I saw this man walking by after waiting for a long time. I said, "Excuse me sir, can you tell me if the <u>burst</u> has yet passed." I did not think that bus was the correct pronunciation.

Well the man laughed at me until the tears ran down his face. I could not understand why he was laughing. Still laughing he replied, "Yes, me dear, the BURST already gone." Of course my brother laughed at me and told the rest of the family when we returned home. I then acquired the name 'Miss BURST', which stuck to me for a very long time.

One of my senior sisters who was married and lived away from home, suddenly returned home, after her husband died after a short illness. She had two children, a girl who was the same age as me and a boy of approximately three to four years old. He was a very handsome boy. My father added another bedroom to the house to accommodate them. To me, at that point in time, she was much like the story of the prodigal son. I must confess that I did not like the idea at the time. She took over much of the duties that my mother used to perform. She said she was giving my mother a rest, but I saw it as helping herself, and her children. She was very selfish; always she would beat me if her daughter and I had a disagreement. Even if her daughter was wrong and I was right, she would slap me! Another thing she did that I hated was that she took over the cooking. She would make sure that she and her children had more than they could manage to eat when she dished out the dinner. I used to pray for her to find another husband and get married again and go away, taking her children with her!

Eventually my prayers were answered. She fell for this wealthy man who also lost his wife. He would come to the house when my father and mother were not at home. Before they got married something happened which made me very sad. Her son had a fit one night and as we lived in the country, the nearest hospital was several miles away in the town. There was no doctor in the area, and so my parents and my sister tried all kinds of homemade remedies. I can remember my mother wrapping a spoon with a handkerchief and using it to open the boy's mouth, as he was biting his tongue and making it bleed. Unfortunately, the boy died within a very short time after the attack.

Her daughter went to the same school as me. She was a very bright girl. She passed all her exams and went on to high school. She left high school and went on to teachers training college. She later became a teacher. She also taught the piano. It was a pleasure to hear her play the piano. My sister later married this wealthy man and both of them immigrated to England. Needless to say I was very sorry to see her go.

One of my older brothers was just like my father. He would beat my younger sister, brother and me if we were a little naughty. The thing is, we dare not report him to our father, as he would just give us another beating for being naughty. He would shout at us just like Father did and generally he was "a second father." I also prayed for him to get married.

My prayers were answered when he fell for the pastor of a small Pentecostal church in the adjoining district. He suddenly became a Christian, and would no longer shout at us. He would be off to church almost every night, and certainly every Sunday. When the rumour started I did not believe it, as I did not think my brother had the nerve to "chat up" the pastor! Apart from that she was much older than my brother. People would travel for miles to go to her church. She could preach! She could also sing. She had a lovely husky voice. The church was approximately one and a half miles from where we lived. It was situated on a fairly steep hill, which made it possible for us to hear the singing and the music from where we lived.

My father finally heard about the relationship and confronted my brother. Of course my father was outraged. I remember hearing my father saying to my brother, "...Is old enough to be your...mother." There was much argument between my father and my brother about the relationship. Eventually my brother married the pastor. They had four children; all except one are now teachers. They have a lovely big house, and are living comfortably. After the marriage, my brother left the church, but his wife is still a pastor in another district, as they left the district where they met.

My first experience of falling in love happened when I was approximately nine or ten years of age. I fell head-over-heels in love with my wealthy neighbour's son who was the same age as me. The problem was, he didn't know. I could not bring myself to tell him, although I am sure he guessed. He was a very good looking boy, with a smooth silk complexion, and lovely straight black hair. He was extremely quiet, and loved his grandmother very much. His grandmother lived alone in a small house, part of which was converted into a small grocery shop that she managed. The house/shop was located close to the main road, approximately ten minutes' walk from where I lived. My "boyfriend" lived on top of the hill in the family house which was a large plantation house, on acres of land, on which they cultivated all kinds of tropical fruits for export. The fruits were harvested by local men, packed in boxes and left by the side of the road. Large trucks would collect the boxes of fruits at intervals. They also cultivated sugar cane which was cut by the locals. They had their own sugar mill and would manufacture hundreds of tins of wet sugar which was then sold to market traders. A part of the property was used for rearing animals. They had lots of cows, horses, mules, chickens, and hundreds of ducks. Of all the animals, the ducks were my favourite. I would sit on the stone wall and watch them swim in the duck pond for hours. I was fascinated by their webbed feet!

My "boyfriend" was a great whistler. He could whistle any type of song. He had to go past my house to visit his grandmother, and to and from school and Sunday school. As soon as I heard his whistling, I would dash into my mother's bedroom, half close the wooden louvre windows, leaving a gap just wide enough to enable me to see him clearly. The closer he got to the house, the faster and louder my little heart would beat! When he was out of window sight, I would creep out and, making sure noone was around, I would stand at the gate and watch him walking and whistling along down the track which runs through the large field. His

whistle grew fainter and fainter as he got closer and closer
to his grandmother's. On his way from his grandmother, my
louvre window ritual would be repeated. On his way back,
I could only see him for a short distance from my mother's
bedroom window, as the trees would obscure my vision as he
whistled along the path up the hill. I soon found a solution
to that problem. I would creep out of the bedroom and into
the outside toilet! I would then stand on the toilet seat and
peep through a hole which I had made. From my peep hole
I could see him until he went through the large wooden gate
which leads to the large plantation house in which he lived.
This was a daily ritual. Until this day he doesn't know how I
felt about him.

 After he left university, he immigrated to England,
where he married an English (white) woman. If only I had
had the courage to tell him how much I loved him, perhaps,
who knows, today I would be Mrs… In my day, class was
not a problem. The reality of rich and poor, upper class,
middle class, low class, black, white, not so black, brown, as
people who had a light colouring was called, but there was
no problem. Everybody just got along. Chinese, Indians,
West Indians, everybody just got on with their lives. It was
like one "happy family". The problem was with the kids. As
always kids will be kids. If a kid was from a wealthy family,
and another was from a very poor family who could not
afford to send their kid to school in shoes, the kid from the
wealthy family would make fun of the poor kid. That was
as far as class, and colour went. Thank God that I have seen
both sides of the coin. The sixties on the one hand, and the
nineties on the other, and if I had a choice, I would choose
to live in the sixties! An era of discipline and respect.

Then there was this other family that lived opposite our kitchen. They consisted of wife and husband, three children and grandmother. They were extremely poor, the grandmother was deaf and dumb, but they were all very light in complexion. Almost white with light straight hair. The mother's hair went down to the middle of her back! The eldest daughter, who was one of my best friends, had lovely long black hair which she usually plaited into two, and just let it hang. Although I had liked the family, there was one thing that I hated, my mother never closed the kitchen door when she was cooking. I think the reason was to allow the smoke which was given off by the wood fire to escape and to allow oxygen to come in through the open door. Their family would always watch through the rows of mango and breadfruit trees to see when my mother finished cooking. To make sure that they didn't miss our dinner time, the older son would climb to the top of a breadfruit tree where he could get a bird's-eye view of our kitchen! As soon as my mother removed the pots from the fire, this boy would appear on the step of the kitchen with a "message" from his mother. The message usually went something like this "Miss. Fan, Mumma say fi tell you say him a beg you little salt Ma" (my mother say she is begging you a little salt), or "Mamma say him a beg you little oil Ma." (Mother say she is begging you a little oil), or "Mamma say him a beg you a stick of matches Ma" (mother say she is begging you a stick of matches), or "Mamma say him a beg you little sugar Ma." (Mother say she is begging you a little sugar).

They knew that my mother would never say no, and that apart from getting what he came to beg, Mother would always give him some of the dinner, and also give him some to take home for the rest of the family! My elder brother, sister and I did not like this. We thought it was going a bit too far. Not one lot of dinner, but two lots gone. We thought that we would get a lot less on our plate. We were pleasantly surprised to find that this was not the case. My mother always cooked extra because she knew that this boy would always turn up. God bless her soul. Sometimes this boy would change his "begging routine", by coming over before Mother finished cooking, and would deliberately "forget" his hat, then when he saw that my mother had finished cooking, he would appear with this excuse, "Miss Fan you see me lef me hat ober ya ma? [Miss Fan, have you seen my hat that I left over here?]" My brother, sister, and I would give him such a nasty look. If looks could kill, that boy would be dead!

As children, my elder brother, sister and I would bet one penny as to what the begging message would be when we saw him striding through the high grass and shrubs towards our kitchen. Sometimes we won, sometimes we lost. This pass the message routine would happen every day of the week. Whenever my sister, brother and I saw this boy, we would shout out at him, "Hello, Mumma say," and make a run for it as he was much older and bigger than we were. If I had to write an EPITATH on the tombstone of my beloved mother it would read:,

HERE LIES THE REMAINS OF FRANCIS SHAW, A LOVING, CARING, KIND, RELIGIOUS MISSIONARY OF THE MOST HIGH GOD, WHO HAS COMPLETED HER PURPOSE HERE ON EARTH, AND IS GONE TO BE WITH HER HEAVENLY FATHER.

Likewise if I had to write an epitath on the tombstone of my
father, it would read:

HERE LIES THE REMAINS OF ADOLPHUS SHAW,
A FIRM, NO-NONSENSE DISCIPLINERIAN.

The father of this family was almost always drunk. He worked
as a lumberjack and was away from home a lot. People in the
neighbourhood would be happy when he was not around.
As soon as he was home for a break from wood cutting,
he would spend the money in the rum bar. He would get
drunk, and was often seen lying by the side of the road. A
lot of times he would be carried home by a passer-by. In his
drunken state he could be heard cursing and shouting at the
family for hours! This was extremely disturbing as this was a
very quiet Christian neighbourhood. Eventually he left the
area to take up residence in one of the towns. The entire
community was very happy when he left.

There were four interesting characters living in the
neighbourhood when I was a child. One was a grandmother
who was deaf and dumb. She walked on the sides of her feet,
and was always shabbily dressed. She looked at people with
a piercing stare that was quite scary. She would roam around
the districts with a basket on her head, and would just walk
into people's plantations and help herself to fruits, yams,
and bananas, whatever she fancied. She would enter people's
plantation and dig up freshly planted yam heads before they
had time to settle in the ground! She would collect these
and then make a wood fire in the yard at nights and cook
the yam heads on the open fire in an iron pot. She would sit
around the fire and sing! It was very fascinating to watch the

outline of her figure in the flickering light of the wood-fire. In the moonlight I would sit on the veranda and watch her for hours. I would try to imitate her singing. As soon as my elder sister and brothers heard her "singing" they would say, "I wonder whose yam heads "Sally" is cooking now?"

The next day, the farmer whose plantation she took the yam heads from would arrive at her house to complain to her daughter or her son-in-law. The daughter would tell her not to do it, but her son-in-law would give her a good beating! I would feel very sorry for her. She would scream very loud, and because she was deaf, the screams sounded muffled, which made it sound as if she was being murdered!

This old lady would pay us a visit when noone was at home, and help herself to my father's ripe coffee beans. She would then process the coffee beans and sell them. I can remember my father would get very cross when he returned home to find all his ripe coffee beans gone! He would shout out something along these lines, "That dam deaf woman was here today, all me coffee beans are gone." My father never complained to her son-in-law because he knew that he would beat her.

There was this other old lady who lived in this small one bedroom bungalow which was very close to the main road. She was half mad, and would sit on the stone wall which separated her property from the main road. She was also shabbily dressed, and would shout swear words at anyone that went by. Adults and children! Sometimes she would throw stones at people. One almost took their life in their hands when they went past her bungalow. I was terrified to go past her house. The problem was it could not be avoided as it was right beside the main road which I had to pass

to go to school, shops and Sunday school. I also had to go
past when I visited my grandfather! Sometimes it would
be a case of "dodge the stones". If I saw her sitting on the
wall, my little heart would beat very fast as I was terrified
of her. I would then pause for a moment, then run as fast
as I could past her. I would call my action "pick up speed".
Sometimes she would hide behind her half closed curtains
in her bungalow, and as soon as anybody went by, she would
rush out and shout or swear at them. Sometimes she would
dash out through her gate and chase children down the
road. I have never heard that she had hurt anyone. On my
way from school, my school friends and I would stop just
before we got to her gate to "pick up speed". We would then
run as fast as we could, so by the time she came out from her
bungalow, we would be long gone!

People used to say Alice was not as mad as she would
have you believe, she behaves like that to prevent people
picking her fruits! Her small bungalow was situated on a
large plot of very fruitful land. Looking back on the situation
now, I tend to believe that this was the case.

The third character was another fairly old woman,
slightly younger than the second character. She also lived
alone in a fairly big bungalow, on a large plot of land
which had lots of fruits and sugarcanes. Her bungalow was
also close to the main road. The good thing was that her
bungalow was obscured by the tall sugarcanes. She was quite
mad. She too was always shabbily dressed. She would sit on
her veranda, and would just shout swear words when people
went by. I had to pass her bungalow quite often because,
as in the case of the second character, I had to pass when I
went to school, Sunday school, and shops, when I followed

my mother to the local market. Because of the fact that her veranda was almost obscured by the sugarcanes, she would depend on sound, rather than sight, to tell her that someone was going by. I would remove my shoes before I got to her gate, and ran as fast as I could.

The last of the four characters was a middle-aged man. I hasten to add that he was not mad. He was a shoemaker by trade. He had his little shoemaking shop by the main road, and he was rather nice. The interesting thing about him was the music he made with his shoemaking hammer as he beat on the leather with which he was working. He also had a lovely voice. As he beat on the leather, he would make music, and then sing to the beat! As a child, I can remember my school friends and I would stand and listen to this shoemaker's "music" and singing on our way home from school, or when we went to the grocery shop. He had a lovely voice and sang along to the music made by his shoemaking tools.

Before I move on, I must tell this bit about my father. My father told me that he had lived in Cuba for a number of years. He was repatriated along with others back to Jamaica. He spoke fluent Spanish and would try to teach me a few words. He also told me that he fought in the 1914 war. When my father was in a good mood, he would sit on the veranda if the moon was shining, as we did not have electricity, and he would tell us all kinds of stories. Mostly he would tell us ghost stories. The one that stuck in my mind is the one about this young man who liked a lot of pretty girls. "One night," said my father, "this young man was coming home very late, and there was no electric lighting on the road. He saw this 'lady' (ghost) walking ahead of him. The more he tried to catch up with this 'lady', the faster the "lady" walked. He kept talking to her, but could not quite see her face. Eventually, he got to his house. The 'lady' was still ahead of him. He was always one who liked his ladies to have nice white teeth! So he said to the lady, 'you can come in and spend the night, but only if you have nice teeth.' The ghost suddenly stopped and turned around, grinned and said 'Teeth like these?' Of course there was no flesh on the face, just the skeleton." My father said that young man screamed and dashed into his house. Since then he was a changed person. No more late nights, and no more chasing of pretty women. As a child, my older brothers, sister and I loved to hear my father's ghost stories. The problem was when it was time to have our wash before going to bed. As there was no proper bathroom, we had to wash outside, behind the bungalow with lighting from a lamp! If there was a strong wind the lamp would blow out! We would then think that a ghost had blown out the lamp. I would scream my head off and run in the house half washed!

My mother became very sick, and had to be admitted to hospital, where it was necessary for her to undergo an operation. She was later sent home from hospital, but her condition deteriorated. She eventually became bed bound, and was nursed mainly by my widowed sister. I would burst into tears every time I saw my mother. Eventually my elder brothers and sisters came to the conclusion that it would be better if I went to live with one of my older sisters who lived in the town, as they could not bear to see me so upset. I was very reluctant to go, but I had no choice as I was the youngest of ten children.

I was well looked after by my sister. She worked as a cook for a very wealthy white family. The husband of this family was the accountant for a large sugar company.

I must have been about sixteen years old when my sister, with whom I was living, decided that it was time that I found myself a job. I wanted to go to be trained as a nurse, but my sister could not afford the fees. She got me a job where she worked as nanny to the baby of her employers. The problem was she did not tell her employers that we were related! She told me not to call her sister while we were on the job. The trouble with that was that I had always called her sister... That was the way it was in those days. The younger children could not call their elder sister or brother by their Christian names. It must always be sister... or brother... I was therefore put under extreme pressure to try to remember not to say sister... when I wanted to call her in the presence of our employers. I sometimes forgot and called her sister, but luckily our employers did not catch on!

I never forgot the day that I was almost electrocuted! As I was brought up in the country, I never had much experience with electricity. I was almost ignorant of the dangers. This day in question, the electric bulb blew in the room that I used to wash and iron the baby's clothes. For some unknown reason, I stood on a chair and removed the bulb. Then I pushed my finger in the socket! I had an electric shock which went through my entire body. It was by the grace of God that I was not killed. That was my first bad experience as an employee!

The second, and most terrible experience that I had on that job was the day when my sister and I got home from work to find a telegram which read, "Mother is dead." I cried so much, I just could not contain myself. The dreadful thing about this situation was when my sister told me to cry as much as I could now because I have to go to work tomorrow, and she doesn't want me to cry on the job when she tells her employer that her mother is dead! She suggested that I try to stay away from the presence of the employers as much as I could, because she couldn't afford to lose her job! Can you imagine? The following day we both went to work. I kept going to the toilet and to the washroom to have a quick cry, then I would wipe my tears and try to pretend that all was well! I cannot explain how I felt, not only that day, but for quite some time. My sister was given time off from work to go to my mother's funeral, but I could not go. I had to continue to work and keep up the pretence. I wanted to just leave the job so that I could go to my dear beloved mother's funeral, but my sister would not agree. She was so afraid that she would lose her job.

After some time had passed, I left the job because I had made up my mind that, come what may, I would not miss the tombing of my mother. On the day of Mother's tombing, I cried so very much. I was sad, bitter and angry. I am convinced that Mother knew the reason why I was not at her funeral. God bless her spirit.

I met my first boyfriend when I was approximately seventeen to eighteen years of age. He was a twenty-four year-old half Cuban, half Jamaican, approximately five feet seven inches tall, dark, and strikingly good-looking. He was always well dressed, with well-groomed black curly hair. He had a good job, and lived in his own rented apartment in the centre of town. He had what I thought was the prettiest bicycle in town. His unique bicycle was decorated with lots of different coloured lights, which all lit up at night. There was also another addition to this bicycle, such as the bell which played music. In those days a well-decorated bicycle was a status symbol, very much the same as a certain make of car is today. My boyfriend's name was Glenroy, affectionately called "Glen". We were very much in love, but at the back of my mind, I always felt that I was not the only girl in town who was in love with him. He was so very handsome.

We had lots of good times together. He was a great lover of the movie, and a very good dancer. At least twice during weekdays, he would call to collect me to take me to a movie, the morning and afternoon of that particular day could not go quickly enough for me! I would literally count the hours. I would have butterflies in my stomach for that entire day. I would go the hairdresser, have a facial, paint my nails, and I would often top it all with a new dress. I would be always ready in good time before Glen came to call for me. The main reason for my getting ready early was because I loved sitting in the back rows of the balcony. These seats were always occupied by young lovers. They were fairly dark, and therefore young lovers could have a kiss and a cuddle without attracting much attention. Saturday nights were special. That's when we would go dancing at our favourite night-club called Chicago After Midnight. Preparing for Saturday night was very exciting. I would ask Glen beforehand which dress I should wear. He often preferred "H" line, off the shoulder, with very wide skirt. This was the fashion that caught the eyes in those days. This kind of dress would be worn with a very wide stiff petticoat which was made from a net material, or calico, which would then

be very heavily starched. I preferred the calico petticoat.
It stood out under the wide skirt better. I would soak my
calico petticoat in what seemed like gallons of starch made
from cassava. I would then hang the petticoat on the clothes
line, pinned upside down along the hem with several clothes
pegs to allow it to dry in shape. When the petticoat was
dry, it looked just like at tent! I had a 36, 26, 36 figure, so I
looked stunning in "H" line, which meant that the waist of
the dress was pinched in to the measurement of the waist.
I very often had my hair cut very short, worn with large
hoop earrings. I would then paint my toenails bright red, as
my outfit would be worn with red or black sandals, called
"toe sandals". These were scanty sandals, which only had a
strap which fastened around the heels, and a strap which
enclosed the big toe. The sandals had very flat heels, which
made them ideal for dancing rock and roll!

We usually went dancing in a group of six, my two
girlfriends and their boyfriends, Glen and me. Glen and I
were very good dancers. Rock and roll was the order of the
night. Our favourite rock singer was the great Elvis Presley.
When Glen and I took to the dance floor, the whole crowd
would stop dancing and gather round us, clapping, cheering
and screaming. This made us feel quite elated, and in total
command of the dance floor. We would then make up extra
moves which were not in our routine. Luckily for us it all
went well. At the end of the dance everybody would offer
to buy us drinks or patties. We would sip cold fruit drinks,
occasionally stopping to eat the odd plastic plate of curry
goat and rice. We would dance the night away, returning
home in the early hours of the morning. A lot of times I was
locked out, and would return home to find that I was unable

to get in. I would go and sleep at one of my girlfriends'. It was not an ideal situation, but as far as I was concerned, it was worth it, just to be out with Glen.

The bottom fell out of my world when one of my girlfriend's told me that Glen was cheating on me. At the beginning I did not want to believe it, but this was told to me several times. I felt shattered. I eventually plucked up the courage and confronted Glen with the allegations. He flatly denied the whole thing. Other friends told me what my girlfriend had told me that it is true that Glen was cheating on me. One even went as far as to tell me that the other "girl" in question was a middle-aged school teacher. She went on to inform me that she had heard a rumour that Glen and this woman were planning to get married! I felt that not only had the bottom fallen out of my world, but that my whole world had caved in! I began to feel quite uneasy in Glen's company. My love for Glen had suddenly turned to hate. Even then I did not want to accept what now appears to be true. I asked him again about the allegations, again he denied it all. I gave him every opportunity to tell me the truth. I told him that if he found someone else who he loved more than he loved me, I would understand, and that I would be hurt to start with but then I would get over it. Of course, that was not the truth, but I just wanted to hear it from his lips that he indeed had another "girl". As it turned out it was a woman almost old enough to be his mother!

The allegations just would not go away. Another friend told me where the woman taught, and also were she lived. One night Glen should have called round to take me to the movie. He did not turn up. That is not like Glen to forget a date with me. I felt confused. My mind began to work overtime. In my confused state, I was trying to think what was the best thing to do? Do I go round to his place to check him out? Or do I go round to the address that my friend gave me and told me that that was where the woman that Glen was cheating on me with lived! After a long hard think, I decided to go round to the address of the woman. The address was a few streets away from where I lived. Under normal circumstances it would take me a matter of approximately fifteen to twenty minutes to walk the distance, but in this abnormal circumstance, it took me what seemed like hours to walk the relatively short distance.

I eventually arrived at the address! My knees were shaking, my heart was racing. I stood outside the gate for what seemed like a very long time. I was trying desperately to pull myself together. All kinds of thoughts were racing through my mind. Should I go in? What if I went in and Glen was not there? If I did go in what would I say to this woman if she came to the door? I kept pacing up and down outside the woman's gate. I was outside that gate for what seemed like hours, trying to figure out how to deal with what has now become a very tricky situation.

I suddenly plucked up enough courage to open the gate and went in. I climbed the steps that led up onto the veranda, and I suddenly found myself confronted with the front door of this woman's apartment. I knocked on the door, although somewhat nervous. Although at this point I felt enough strength and anger that made me feel that I could handle whatever the outcome would be. The light came on and a middle-aged, fair-skinned woman opened the door! "What do you want, little girl?" she said to me.

"Is Glen there?" I said.

"Who are you?" she replied.

"I am Glen's girlfriend," I said.

"Glen" did not tell me that he had a girlfriend," she replied. I shouted at her, "I have heard all about you and Glen," I said. "You are old enough to be Glen's mother! What is Glen doing with an old woman like you"?

At that point she shouted, "Glen, come out here." I almost collapsed on the floor when Glen came out from what must have been her bedroom. She then asked him who this girl was.

The answer that Glen gave I can still hear ringing in my ears as I recall the memory. He said, "Go home, Ann and I are going to be married soon."

I could not believe that I heard what I was hearing. I shouted, "You are a dirty cheating…" Then I turned to the woman and said, "You can have him, the same knife that stick goat is the same knife that stick sheep," meaning that if he cheated on me therefore he will cheat on her. I felt betrayed, angry and dejected.

I never went back to Glen's apartment, and he never came round to see me. The relationship simply died. During that week, and for a very long time after, I felt physically weak. I felt a feeling of complete and utter failure. I could not understand why Glen had done that. I searched myself, but could not find one single area in which I had failed. That gave me some sort of comfort which I held on to during the very painful time of healing.

I refused to date for a very long time. Then my eyes caught this tall, thin, good-looking young man, who went past my house frequently, morning and evening. Then one day, I bumped into him in town and he asked me out. Although I said yes, I would not go to the movie with him. I went home and gave the matter a great deal of thought. Finally, I decided to give it a try. On our first date, Allan was very warm; we held hands and munched peanuts and popcorn as we watched the movie. I think the movie was called *Seven Brides for Seven Brothers*.

During the months that followed, I found that although I had liked Allan very much and he appeared to be in love with me, he did not even try to kiss me! He seemed very shy and unsure of himself. Allan was a very excellent dancer. We would go dancing every Saturday night. His favourite record was 'Rock Around the Clock" by Bill Haley. Oh boy could he move! He could dance on the head of a pin to any rock and roll record. Once we got on the dance floor, everybody would stop dead in the middle of the record and gather around Allan and me, clapping and screaming. We had the complete dance floor to ourselves. After the club closed, in the early hours of the morning, Allan and I would walk home. It was very romantic walking along the quiet streets holding hands with noone in sight, except the occasional road-sweeper. Allan would walk me home to my gate which was a distance of approximately one mile, without even trying to give me a little peck on the cheek!

Allan often came to my gate and handed me a surprise parcel. I would open the parcel to find a new pair of dancing sandals, or a length of dress material. Allan was very kind, although I told him often enough not to buy me these gifts, but Allan would not take no for an answer. Allan would stop giving me the parcels and would hand me a letter instead. I would open the letter to find some money with a note to say

I must go and buy myself a dress or a pair of sandals to wear to the movie or to go dancing.

I went out with Allan for approximately one and a half years. During this time, Allan had never kissed me. I began to worry about this. I told my very close girlfriend about the fact that from the time I had been going out with Allan he never once kissed me. My girlfriend then said to me that if she was in my shoes, she would break off the relationship. It was as if she could read my thoughts! What she said to me was exactly what I was thinking. Although Allan had some very good qualities, it could be very boring being in his company. I was completely baffled. Allan was approximately twenty-three years of age, he looked and acted quite mature, but when he was with me, he seemed quite incapable as to how to handle a girl.

To brag a bit about myself, I was about nineteen years of age, very attractive, brown hair and grey eyes, very light complexion and had a perfect figure of 36, 26, 36. I was also a very good dresser. I had searched and searched, but could not come up with an answer for Allan's attitude towards me!

I finally decided to break off the relationship. It was very difficult to put my thoughts into implementation. I began to break off the relationship gradually by making excuses each time Allan asked me out to the movie or to go dancing. My excuses were so frequent that Allan finally got the message that I did not want to go out with him any longer! After some time he stopped coming around to ask me out.

After two failed relationships, I came to the conclusion that I would give men a miss for a while. I was quite content to go out with my girlfriends and have a good time. The problem was that many times my girlfriends were with their boyfriends, and I felt as though I was getting in the way. Although my girlfriends tried to reassure me that this was not the case, I thought otherwise. Just at the point that I began to feel despondent, I met Claude. He was the son of the minister of my local church. Claude was fairly short and plump (slightly fat). He was of a light complexion, with black wavy hair, and very, very, good-looking. He rode a well-decorated bicycle, which brought back memories of Glen. When I met Claude, it was love at first sight. Our eyes met, and I was transfixed. The beat of my heart multiplied threefold, and I felt a strange weakness at my knees and ankles. I knew immediately that I was in love with Claude. I had an instant feeling of "this is the guy for me" syndrome. At our very first meeting Claude asked if I would go to the movie with him that night. I said, "Yes, I would be delighted." That day, waiting for the time when Claude would call to collect me on the cross-bar of his bicycle was the longest day of my life! Finally, that evening at around seven thirty, there was the long-awaited ring of Claude's musical bicycle bell at my gate. My heart started to pound, and my knees and ankles started to shake. I slightly opened the curtain of my bedroom window, and there he was! Suddenly I plucked up the courage and came out from by bedroom. I waked onto the veranda, down the steps and opened the gate. "Well hello, how are you?" I said, as I was quietly hoping and praying that he would not hear the beat of my heart! The nearness of my body next to his brought on a strange feeling, as though I had known Claude for a very long time. So intense was this feeling that I invited him in, and introduced him to my sister. I had an overwhelming confidence that my sister would approve of him. When I told my sister that Claude's father was the minister of the local church, she appeared very pleased. She shook Claude's hands very warmly and said, "I am very pleased to meet you." I knew then that this time I was onto a winner.

After a brief chat with my sister, we were off to the movie. I was transported on the cross-bar of his bicycle. We sat holding hands throughout the movie. My heart beat so hard, and so fast, that the sound of my heart almost drowned out the sound of the words of the actors and actresses! Claude loved the movie, eating out, going to the ice-cream parlour, where he would mix several different flavours of ice-creams, and going to the river for picnics. I loved going to the river for picnics. There was this large tree which fell in the river and was just left. We would sit on this fallen tree trunk, and just hold hands chatting and laughing! I was quite scared of the river, as I could not swim, but somehow when I was in the company of Claude I felt safe. I still have a treasured photograph that he took of me sitting on the trunk of that very special love tree. Claude was not allowed to go dancing; his father would not let him because of his position in the church. Claude was quite shy. I think the reason for his shyness was because he was not allowed to mix with young people of his own age group, except of course the youngsters in his father's church. He had one sister who was years younger than himself, which did not improve the mixing problem!

I went out with Claude for over three years. During this time I was so much in love with him that I would do almost anything to keep him. He was also desperately in love with me.

The funny thing was history seemed to be repeating itself all over again. During the three years that I went out with Claude, not once did he kiss me properly, just the sisterly peck on the cheek. Neither did he once mention lovemaking! At first I thought, it's because of his religious upbringing. I waited and waited, and waited, and hoped, and kept hoping but, alas, nothing happened. I was totally devastated. I did not want to leave him because I was so much in love with him!

I wanted desperately to talk to someone about it, but could not bring myself to talk to any of my girlfriends. I certainly could not talk to my sister who was my second mum! I was in a real state! A state of "third time unlucky". I could not ask Claude what the problem was, because in my young days, this was just not done. Girls could not take the lead in sex matters. If they did, they were looked upon as cheap. I was at the end of my tether. It was now clearly a case of "take it or leave it". I could not take it, and neither could I leave it! How could I leave Claude? I was still madly in love with him, and apart from being in love; he only lived a few streets away from my house! Although he was not a sexy person, I would be very jealous if I left him and then saw him with another girl.

I finally came to a decision. Although it was a very painful decision, I decided to bear the pain, and to break off the relationship by playing the excuses game. Each time Claude asked me out, I would make up an excuse. I was always going to the hairdresser, or I had a headache, or I had tummy ache. Finally, he clicked that I did not want to go out with him anymore, and he did not like it. I never knew that Claude could get angry. He would come around on his bicycle and just sit there on his bike at my gate, and would refuse to go away if I had made up one of my excuses so as not to go out with him. He just would not stop coming round. He would come round every evening and just sit there on his bike. Sometimes he would ask my sister to talk to me. She wanted to know the reason why I did not want to go out with Claude but, of course, I could not tell her the truth!

Claude's waiting game went on for a very long time. He took it much harder than me. It reached a point where I became almost afraid of Claude. He became quite hostile, and would keep ringing his bicycle bell, and would often shout out my name. The situation became quite embarrassing. The neighbours would come out, and I could see them whispering!

Then I met Anthony. Tony as everyone called him. Tony was quite handsome; he drove an old Ford Anglia, and worked as an accountant at the local textile plant. He was extremely intelligent and was left-handed. He was also very proud. He walked with his head in the air, and with a certain spring in his steps. Tony was much older than me and acted more mature than my former boyfriends. I must confess that it was not love at first sight with Tony. Although I did like him, mainly for educational standard, and the fact that he held such a very good job. When I met Tony he was living with his aunt in the part of town that was referred to as downtown. I never forget the very first time that Tony invited me home to meet his aunt, a silvery-haired old lady, who he lovingly called Aunt Katch. I was very nervous about meeting her, but when I did, I soon realised that there was no need to be fearful. She was a very sweet old lady, who made me feel very much at home, after only a few minutes in her company. She chatted away as though I was in the

family a very long time. I was even more surprised when she
told Tony what a lovely girl I was, and that he must take care
of me!

Something happened at that very first meeting that
made an indelible impression on my mind. I will never
forget that moment. Even as I recall the incident, it is as
fresh in my mind as though it happened yesterday! As I said
goodbye, Tony walked me to the gate, and then he came
out and stooped down in the street, which is a cul-de-sac.
There he remained in the squatting position, as I walked
away up a slight gradient, I kept looking back, and each
time I looked back, I could see him still in the stooping
position, just watching me walking up the gradient towards
the top of the lane, which leads to the main street. At the
top of the lane I turned right, into the main street, and as I
walked out of his sight, I turned back for a last look to see if
he was still stooping there, and I saw him writing something
in the dusty lane!

The next time I saw Tony, he was just bubbling over
with happiness! He told me how he had stooped down and
watched me walk away the other day, after he introduced me
to Aunt Katch. He said he could not take his eyes off me,
just in case, as I walked away home up the gradient. He said
he had never seen a figure like mine. He kept on remarking
about how slim my waistline was. I felt quite flattered. He
then went on to tell me how much he loved me, and that as
he watched me walk away, he knew that I was the girl that
he would marry! He said he wrote in the dust on the lane the
words, "I love you and I am going to marry you." Each time
Tony came to pick me up in his car, Claude would be sitting
on his bike in front of my gate. Each time a confrontation

took place, there would be an unholy war. Claude would shout at Tony, "She is my girl, our relationship is not over yet!" Tony offered to punch Claude at that point Claude went off on his bike. I thought to myself, *Thank God, this is the last time I will have to put up with this warring*, but that was not the case. Claude still kept coming round and the "war of words" continued.

I began to feel quite sorry for Claude. Because he took it so badly he began to lose a lot of weight. Everybody who knew of the break-up would remark how much weight Claude was losing, and how he was fretting over me! I felt quite sorry for him; I almost felt a feeling of guilt. I felt even guiltier when Claude confided in one of his close friends, that I was the very first girl that he had been out with. Claude would just not let go. When he got tired of the war of words with Tony, he would just sit there on his bike and watch me get in Tony's car. Then as soon as Tony drove off, Claude would ride off on his bike behind the car, at great speed, trying to keep up with the car for as long as he could, shouting!

It got to the stage where the situation was getting on my nerves. I would feel quite frightened each time that I looked out of my bedroom window and saw Claude sitting at my gate on his bike. The fear would get worse if I knew that Tony would be coming to pick me up. It became like a soap opera, the neighbours would all come out to watch the drama each time that Tony came round to pick me up.

I finally plucked up the courage to introduce Tony to my sister. At the introduction my sister shook his hands politely and said, "Pleased to meet you." She talked with him for a short time, and then Tony and I went off on our date. During the date, I was somewhat uncomfortable, I kept seeing the semi-cold look in my sister's eyes as she looked Tony over from head to toe. I knew that she did not like him. Having been practically brought up by my sister, I got to know her very well. She doesn't have to speak, I could read her thoughts.

I was not looking forward to going home to hear my sister's comments about what she thought of Tony. Finally, the date ended, and I had to go home to face her comments. Just as soon as I walked through the front door, my sister was waiting for me. Before I could utter a single word she burst out, "I don't like him. He is too proud, two big headed. Walking like his feet can't touch the ground. Don't bring him back here. What happened to you and Claude? Claude is a nice boy, I like Claude." At that moment, I felt as though the whole world had caved in on me. I wanted to scream. If only I could tell her the problem that caused me to break up with Claude!

That night I hardly slept. I kept thinking how I could resolve the situation. The next day, sure enough Claude returned to take up his usual vigil, and Tony returned to pick me up in his car, and the neighbours came out to watch the drama.

I had a very enjoyable night out, but as the time drew near for me to return home, I began to feel a sense of sadness. I knew that my sister would be waiting up for me, and I was not looking forward to what she had in store for me. This time she was asleep when I got home, but as soon as I turned the light on, she flew at me like an angry eagle whose sleep had been disturbed! "You went out again with that boy Tony again, me no tell you say me don't like him.

If you turn woman and won't listen to me, then get out." There was an unholy row. She kept nagging, and nagging. Every time that I began to fall asleep, she shouted something unpleasant about Tony. The next day she kept on at me to get out. I could see that she was not joking from the stare in her eyes! I thought to myself, *My God, what do I do now?*

I decided to talk to Tony about my dilemma. That night Tony picked me up to take me to the movie. When he drove off I said to him, "I don't feel like going to the movie tonight, I have something to discuss with you, would you mind if we went to your place where we could sit in comfort and discuss the matter?" He was so understanding. We drove to his aunt's house where he lived, and went into the living-room where he sat me down, put his arms lovingly around me and said, "Tell me all about it, what is the problem?" At that moment I just burst into tears. I could not stop crying. Tony hugged me so very tenderly, just as a father would hug his tearful child, then he reached into his pocket for a handkerchief and wiped my weeping eyes! For the very first time I felt what it was like to be really loved. He made me feel so comfortable, I just poured out everything.

"Don't worry," he said, "tomorrow we will go room hunting, and I am sure that we will find a nice big front room. I have some money; we will go to McPhail furniture store and get a double bed, dining table and chairs, wardrobe, one easy chair and a dresser (dressing table). We will get some utensils and a cooker." I was just amazed at Tony's reaction to my problem! He made the whole thing seem so easy. Of course I didn't want Tony to buy everything. I had some money for myself, and I decided that I would buy the furniture and that he could pay the rent. We argued nicely for a while, because "Tony" wanted to buy the furniture, utensils and pay the rent! We finally settled for what I wanted, I would buy the furniture and he would pay the rent.

The following day I went room hunting. Someone told me that a lady who lived just around the corner from where I lived had got a big front room to rent. I went to see the lady and, sure enough, she had a very big front room to rent. In those days when one is just starting out, before one graduates to renting an apartment, one would start off by renting a front room. This meant exactly what it said, front room, and the best room in a person's house. The room to the front of the house, and not only that it is at the front of the house, it is also the biggest room in the house. Often one can divide their front room and use half as a bedroom and half as a sitting/dining area. I was very pleased when the lady showed me the front room. I would also have half of the veranda, and half of the kitchen. That meant that I could put my easy chair on the veranda. By so doing, it was almost as though I had an apartment.

There was only one snag, the lady who was renting the front room knew my sister very well. She wanted to know the reason why I was leaving home. When I told her the reason, she asked me to bring Tony round to meet her before she would agree to let me have the room. I brought him round to her and, fortunately, she liked him. Perhaps it was because he turned up driving a car! She sat us down and gave us both a good lecturing. She wanted to know where Tony worked, what work he did, where he lived and all about his parents. For a moment, I thought we were having an interview for a job instead of being a potential tenant for a front room.

When she was satisfied, she said OK and that I could have the room", but before I moved in, she lectured me about cleaning my half of the veranda, keeping my cupboards in the kitchen clean, keeping the shower room clean, not having a lot of friends coming to visit me and, finally, no boyfriends apart from Tony to visit me while I lived at her house. She also wanted one month's rent in advance. That was not a problem. "Tony" was only too willing to put his hand into his pocket, took out his wallet and reel out the pound notes. She gave me the receipt for the rent and we left.

I felt so happy; it is not possible to put my feelings on paper! To try to analyse my feelings, it was a though I had a telephone call to say that I had won one million pounds on the pools!

That night I went out with Tony and stayed out I really did not care how much my sister carried on about going out with Tony. I did not tell her that I had got a room. Not only a room, but a front room with half of a veranda and half of a kitchen! Needless to say when I returned home the morning after the night before, all hell broke loose! She shouted at me, "Not only do you continue to go out with Tony, but you have gone one step further. Now you start to sleep out with him. Next thing you will come in with belly (pregnant). Now you not turning woman, you a woman, and two women can't live under one roof."

I just took it all with a smile. I was not upset, I was not crying. She could not understand why I was so calm. When she saw that I was not upset or crying, she shouted even more. The more she shouted, the calmer I became, because I knew that I have got my front room, and it is just a matter of days until I sorted myself out, and move out!

That same day, I went to town and bought a hand-broom, dustpan, mop, duster, polish for the floor, and other things that I needed to clean the place up before the furniture was delivered. I spent the rest of the day cleaning and polishing my front room, my half of the veranda, and my half of the kitchen. The landlady was very helpful and kind. She had four children: two girls and two boys. I loved the children. They were like my little brothers and sisters. They also liked Tony and me a great deal. They were almost always in my room or around me when I was sitting on the veranda.

I think the next happiest day of my relationship with Tony was the day when he took the day off from work to wait with me at my front-room for my furniture to be delivered. I can still picture the headboard in my mind's eye. There was a painting of a basket of flowers in the centre of the headboard. It was just so very beautiful. Apart from by brand new double bed, there was my new mahogany dining table and four chairs, a beautiful mahogany dresser and easy chair, and mahogany wardrobe. I also bought a wooden deck-chair for my half of veranda. I felt like a full grown young lady!

Problems started when Claude found my new address. Obviously my sister told him where I had moved to and, of course, it wasn't long before he appeared at my gate ringing his bicycle bell, and inquiring whether I had moved there.

Tony put a stop to that when he rented a two bedroom bungalow approximately two miles out of town and moved me there. The bungalow was in its own grounds, which was a fairly large plot, with several fruit trees, and a large garden. It was such a lovely change from living in town where there was always more than one bungalow clustered together on a small plot of land, and a lot of times there were no fruit trees or garden. It was such a joy to walk up to my front door through my very own front gate. The overwhelming joy of having my own veranda and not having to share a kitchen and bathroom was almost too much to contemplate.

With all this unexpected joy I was still not completely without a sense of anxiousness. I was looking over my shoulder whenever I went shopping in town. I was so afraid of bumping into Claude! I was not sure what his reaction would be if we bumped into each other.

Tony put a stop to that by getting me a maid. I could hardly believe my ears when Tony told me that he would get me a maid, and that I didn't have to go shopping in town if I didn't want to. Suddenly I felt what it was like to be the mistress instead of the maid. It was a very good feeling, and I liked the feeling. During the time that Tony was looking for a maid, if I needed groceries that I couldn't get at the local corner shop and had to go into town for, Tony would pay someone, usually a young man, to go and do the shopping or, alternatively, he would arrange with the owner of the grocery shop to have the groceries delivered to me. Tony thought of just about everything that would make me happy.

I never forget the day when this young lady arrived at my bungalow and said to me that her name was Jane, and that she was told that I was looking for a maid. The irony was that she was much older than I was. I sat her down on the veranda, gave her a glass of cold drink, and plucked up the courage to interview her. She was neatly dressed, quietly spoken, and gave me the impression that she was not cheeky.

I hired her, on a trial period of one month. At the end of her probationary period, I would then decide if I would employ her on a permanent basis. She appeared very grateful that I had decided to give her a try. She thanked me, promised to work to the best of her ability and left. After she had gone I was beside myself with happiness! I threw my hands up in the air, and remarked to myself, "Well Gloria, you are stepping up in the world. You have found yourself a mature boyfriend, who has a car, a good job, is well educated, have your own bungalow, and now your own maid." I could hardly contain myself.

That evening when Tony came to see me, I told him that I had hired a maid on a probationary basis. He was very pleased. Then he dropped another bombshell by telling me that from now on I am not going to work for anybody. His wife-to-be 'must not work for nobody'. He was adamant about this statement. I was shell-shocked. Everything seemed to be happening too fast for me to absorb. Just when I thought that was the end of what I would call a string of fortunate happenings, there was more! Tony went on to say he wanted to marry me, and that he would like to move in with me for a short time before we got married to give me the chance to see how I felt about his marriage proposal. Well I was completely lost for words.

Tony was a very proud young man. Although I loved him very much, sometimes I would find his attitude a little overbearing. The thing about Tony is that he would always put his money where his mouth was. That was a quality in him that I loved. Anything to do with finance, he would never say he would do it, and then back down. His word was his bond, and his money was his magic wand.

After a short while, Tony moved into the bungalow with me. At first, it felt quite strange, but I soon got used to having Tony around, as man of the house. One of the things that I enjoyed was taking Tony's lunch to the textile factory where he worked as an accountant. Tony bought me this small motorcycle, and I just loved riding around on it. I loved wearing jean skirts and white blouses. I would wear the blouse outside of the skirt; make a knot with the two ends of the blouse to the front, leaving my midriff showing, the fashion in those days. I was a real tom-boy. I would secure the lunch basket firmly to the back of the motorcycle, and ride at great speed, hair flying in the wind, dressed in jeans, blouse and sandals, and dark glasses. On my arrival at the factory, which was completely fenced in with very high fencing, a high iron gate at the entrance with a small guard-house, as soon as the guard heard the roaring of the motorcycle, he would come out to the gate, "Good morning, Miss G, Mr. Higgins lunch Ma?" give me a big grin, open the gate and took the lunch basket. "I will phone Mr. Higgins and tell him that you are here, Ma. There was always a crowd of young men and women outside the factory gate, hoping to get a job. They would come up to me and say "Miss G, can you ask your husband if he can help me to get a job, Ma?" After a short while "Tony" would come striding down the pathway to collect his lunch. He would open the gate, give me a sweet smile, a peck on the cheek, and tell me, "Thanks". All the unemployed young people would crowd around him, begging him to help them to get a job. I felt quite sorry for them.

A near accident put a stop to me riding the motorcycle permanently. One day I was returning home from the factory, after taking Tony's lunch. I was riding at great speed, as I approached a bend on the left of the road; I was travelling too fast, and almost went into a large tree. I was so shaken up; I managed to stop the bike inches before it went into the tree. That was the end of my motorcycle riding! From then onwards, I took Tony's lunch by minicab or minibus.

There would be times when there was a shortage of certain foods, such as cooking oil, salted cod fish, rice, salted mackerel and kerosene oil. People would have to travel miles to an area where the items were available. Whenever there was a shortage, I never had a problem. Young men would come to my house early in the morning and queue up to offer their services. That is to ride their bicycles to wherever they could get the food stuff for me, hoping that in return my husband would be able to help them to get a job at the textile factory where he worked!

Jane was an excellent maid, or so it seemed, until items of clothing started to disappear. Tony's shirts started diminishing, then his socks started to vanish, then my bras and panties disappeared one by one. I was too scared to confront Jane about the missing items. The crunch came when one of my favourite bras vanished. I got Tony to confront Jane about the missing items. On the day of the confrontation, I was very proud of Tony. He handled the situation so well. He did not mince his words. He simply called the maid and told her that she had been taking items of both his clothing and Miss G's panties and bras. He went on to tell her point blank, that she was a thief! He concluded the confrontation by telling her, in no uncertain terms, to pack her bags and get out before he called the police. Well, I could hardly believe my ears. The maid hung her head in shame, started crying and replied, "I did not do it, Sa [Sir]." Tony just shouted at her to, "Get out and don't come back." She gathered her things and went. That was the end of Jane. That was also my first unhappy experience in my new home.

My second unhappy experience was when one of my nieces, who was a high school student, a very bright girl, started to bunk off from school, and would come to my home, and just lay on the floor and sleep all day. She begged me not to tell her mother. I was torn between loyalty to my niece and the loyalty to my older sister. The young girl was about sixteen years of age. She would not tell me what the problem was. After some time had passed, I realised that she was pregnant!

My stay in what I thought was my ideal home, was short lived, when frogs started invading the bungalow! The veranda was quite low to the ground, which made it easily accessible to frogs. They would simply leap up unto the veranda. I would find them under my bed at times. I was in a continual state of "fear of the frogs". I was always screaming at the sight of frogs invading the bungalow! I would even find them in the bathroom, and even in the kitchen. It was a real nightmare. I began to wonder if that was the reason why the owner of the bungalow packed his bags and went off to England!

Most days Tony would come home from work and would find me sitting under a mango tree which was situated at the entrance of the bungalow. I was too terrified to stay there.

I never forget the day when I decided to take a midday nap. I was awakened by the croaking of a frog under my bed. I screamed so loud the neighbour came running over to see what was wrong! He found me bracing myself so close to the wall on top of my bed; I almost pushed myself right through the wall. He managed to get the frog out from under my bed after what seemed to me like hours of trying! That was the last daytime nap I had in that bungalow.

When Tony heard of my plight, being the type of man that he was, he decided that it was time we moved back into town. The very next day Tony started house hunting. It wasn't long before he found a beautiful bungalow. This was a very large family house divided into two dwellings. The landlord, his wife and daughter lived in one half of the building, and Tony and I lived in the other half.

I was extremely happy to move back to civilization! The fear of looking over my shoulder for Claude had completely vanished. I felt quite secure with Tony around. I was quite sure that after a few confrontations with Tony Claude realised that Tony was not a guy to mess with!

All that was missing to complete my newfound happiness was an honest maid. Tony, myself, friends and the youngsters who usually hang out at the factory where Tony worked, put the word out that I was looking for another maid. The solution came in an unexpected way, in the form of my older sister. One day while she was visiting me, she said, "G, I hear that you are looking for a maid."

I replied, "Yes, I am."

She then replied, "Well, I am not ashamed to come and work for you, I need the money."

I was quite taken aback. I hesitated for a while, then I said, "Are you sure you want to come and work for me?"

"Yes," she said, "when do you want me to start?" she replied.

Again I hesitated, and then I replied, "If you are sure that you really want to work for Tony and me, you can start at the beginning of the month."

"Fine," she replied. "What salary do you pay?" We agreed a figure, and that was that. She continued chatting away, only this time she appeared very happy.

When she left that evening, after she offered to cook dinner, I felt quite funny. I just felt that it was not right for my elder sister to come to work for me. I started to wonder what the rest of the family, her husband, and her children would say about her coming to work for Tony and me. Would they think that I was taking advantage of her because she was less well-off than me? All kinds of thoughts started going through my mind. I loved my sister dearly. The family always said, "I am her mother." I could not bear to think that they would think that I was taking advantage of her! I felt very uneasy about the situation. Although she was the one who offered, I thought, would the family see it that way? I also thought, *Please God, Help!* I was very young and inexperienced, and I honestly did not know how to handle the situation.

When Tony arrived home from work that evening, I tried very hard to conceal my feelings about the situation. After he had dinner, I plucked up the courage to tell him that Aunt B, as we affectionately called my sister, offered to come to work for us. Tony didn't seem to mind. "Good," he replied, "At least we know that we now have someone we can trust." I began to feel a bit more comfortable. During the rest of the month Aunt B would come around quite regularly to help me with the housework. She was more like a mother instead of a sister. She was an excellent cook and when it came to washing and ironing, she was simply the best! Sometimes she would even take Tony's lunch to the factory where he worked. She was just wonderful. As the days went by, I began to feel quite comfortable with her around doing the housework. I suddenly thought perhaps I had made a good decision after all. She even took me under her wing and gave me a few lessons about cooking and shopping. I suddenly began to count the days to the end of the month in anticipation of her starting work at the beginning of the month. Finally, the big day arrived. It was a Monday morning. I remember it as clear as if it was yesterday. She stepped up unto the veranda bright and early. "G," she shouted, "I am here." I opened the door to be greeted by her broad smile. "Good morning," she said, "what do you want me to do first?"

I replied "Cook some breakfast for you, Tony and me." I did not have the problem of showing her where things were kept. She knew exactly where everything was. She just got right on with it. That was the best breakfast I had tasted for a long time. Not because it was cooked any differently from the other ones she had cooked, it was the thought that this was now on a permanent basis.

I was very happy, but Aunt B appeared even happier. After she had cooked the breakfast, I took Tony's to the factory where he worked. When he came out to collect the breakfast, guess what I said? "This one is special, cooked by the one and only Aunt B."

Tony gave a very broad smile and replied "Well this is not the first time that I have tasted Aunt B's cooking!" I could not help but notice that he had an extra spring in his step as he walked away up the path which led to the entrance door of the factory. He was very, very happy. I could almost hear him whisper, *thank God, my wife's maid problem is over.* I knew that was exactly what Tony would say. He was that kind of a loving and caring husband. I could read his mind like an open book.

Not very long after Aunt B started to work for Tony and me, Tony not only "popped the question", but was very adamant that it was time we got married. Although I loved Tony very much, I was not sure whether I was ready for marriage. All my girlfriends were still single, going to nightclubs with their boyfriends and just having a good time. Although Tony was very loving and caring, he had a slightly bossy side to his character which I was not quite sure that I could handle. I was now in a bit of a quandary; one that I was not sure that I could get myself out of. "If only my mother was still alive," I thought, I could talk to her. I certainly could not talk to my older sister who brought me up after Mum's death. I knew exactly what her reply would be, "Don't marry that big-head, show-off boasty boy. Him walking like him foot can't touch ground. I don't like him."

I decided to talk to Aunt B about the matter. On day after lunch as we sat on the veranda, I decided that that was a good time to discuss the matter. I asked her what did she thought about me marrying Tony? She was over the moon with happiness! "Marry him," she replied. "He has a good job; he is well educated, has a car, has money and treats you right. I know the others won't like him, but don't mind them, it's your life." I pondered her reply over, and over in my mind, suddenly I came to the conclusion that I agreed with her. After all, the only person who I would worry about pleasing was my mum, and she was dead! I decided that when Tony came home from work that evening I would tell him that I would marry him. That evening, after supper, I told Tony that I would marry him! I cannot find words to put in writing the expression of the joy that appeared on his face. He was beside himself with happiness. He squeezed me so tight; he almost squeezed the life out of me! Then came a barrage of, "I love you, I will make you very happy, I will be faithful to you, you will not regret making this decision etc."

Then Tony dropped another bombshell. He told me that he wanted a bigger apartment, a whole house for us to live in. He said he didn't want to share his matrimonial home with anyone. The "house hunting program" was on once more. Finding houses to rent was not a great problem in those days, as the middle and upper classes of people would readily deal in real estate, where they would have a number of houses for rent. It was not long before we found a beautiful house in the centre of town, on a quiet street; we moved house. After we had settled in I decided it was time to tell the family, including my dreaded older sister!

Tony wanted to tell his old aunt (Aunt Katch) who also brought him up when his mum died. Aunt Katch was much older than my sister, therefore, we both agreed to tell her the good news first. One Sunday evening, after dinner, we got in the car and went to see Aunt Katch. We all sat on the veranda, which was over-shadowed by a large mango tree; the bunches of ripe ones swayed in the cool gentle evening breeze. I could not help but wonder whether this was the calm before the storm. I was not quite sure what Aunt Katch would say about the proposed marriage. Although she appeared to like me quite a lot, and had been very kind to me, I did not know her long enough to be able to come to any conclusion of how she would react to the news of her son marrying me!

Tony chatted for a while about our new home, about how much he loved me, and other subjects, before he dropped the clanger of his proposed marriage to me. I was pleasantly surprised at the reaction of the old lady. I need not have worried. She was very happy! She gave me a very tender hug, just as my own mum would, if she was still alive! Then she went on to caution Tony about treating this lovely young girl right. I felt a sense of happiness, and guilt. Happiness because of the way she reacted, and guilt because I misjudged her reaction wrongfully. Well, the rest of the evening was a piece of cake. Conversation just flowed between the three of us. I felt secure knowing that Aunt Katch approved of her son marrying me; and, as a bonus, she was already on my side. I felt like a million dollars! The rest of the evening we sat drinking iced drinks and generally discussing the wedding plans. When it was time for Tony and I to leave she reminded Tony of her warning. "Take good care of her," were her parting words. As Tony and I drove home, after what we thought was a very delightful evening, we chatted happily about the old lady's reactions to our wedding plans, and I reminded him lovingly about Aunt Katch's warnings. The words of a very wise old lady. The perfect ending to a beautiful evening!

My next hurdle was what I thought was the most difficult. That was to tell my sister, who brought me up, about my wedding plans. Needless to say that night I hardly slept a wink. I was awake almost all night thinking how I was going to break the news of my intended wedding to

Tony. That was the longest night of my life! Finally, I heard the cockerels crowing, and the birds singing, which signalled the break of day. Shortly after the birds stopped singing and the cockerels stopped crowing, the rays of the sun came streaming through my bedroom window, as if to say, wake up." I slowly got myself out of bed, feeling slightly light-headed from lack of sleep. I made my way to the bathroom and tried to wake myself up with a cold shower!

When Aunt B arrived for work at eight o'clock, I had already finished cooking breakfast. "What happened? Why are you up so early, G, something wrong?"

"Have your breakfast," I replied, "then take Tony's to the factory. I will tell you all about it when you return." Aunt B looked a bit worried. I put her mind at rest by telling her she had done nothing wrong, it was just something that was bothering me, and I hadn't slept well. A smile came to her face, "OK then," she said. "Tell me about it when I return from the factory." Before she left I cautioned her not to tell Tony that I was worried. She agreed not to, and left to catch the taxi with Tony's breakfast.

On her return from the factory, she hurried into the diningroom where I was still sitting around the dining-table. I honestly don't know how long I had sat there after finishing my breakfast. It must have been at least two hours. She had an anxious look on her face. "Well, tell me about it," she exclaimed. I was somewhat glad for the opportunity to pour out my heart to Aunt B. It gave me the opportunity to rehearse what I had planned to say to my elder sister.

At the end of my rehearsal, Aunt B replied, "Is that what you have been worrying yourself about? Don't I tell you before that it is your life, and that Tony is OK? Is you going to live with Tony or is Ethlin? You have time to be worrying yourself about what Ethlin is going to think about your intended husband. Cheer up, and stop worrying yourself. Ethlin is old already; she has gone past the marrying stage. She has never married, and she doesn't want to get married. Are you going to let Ethlin cause you to become an old maid [Left on the shelf]?" Aunt B's words were a tonic to my system. I thought about what she had said, and it was not long before I agreed with every word.

At that point of my life Aunt B was what I thought a very good substitute for my mother. I honestly think those would be the exact words my mother would use or words slightly similar if she was alive. Well, after her motherly chat, she made a cup of her special coffee, which activated my senses to see things her way.

That evening, with the adrenalin still running high, when Tony returned home from work, after supper, I felt that I was ready to face my senior sister. I casually said to Tony, "Let's go and see Eth and tell her of our wedding plans!

He paused for a moment, wide-eyed and mouth slightly opened, he replied, "Are you sure you want to go this evening?"

"Yes," I replied. Within my heart I kept saying *Please don't debate the matter, hurry up before the adrenalin stops flowing.*

"OK then," he replied. "If you are quite sure that you are ready to face Eth, I am ready because I am not afraid of a damn soul!" Little did he know how those words were like music to my ears. I knew that when I turned up on my sister's doorstep accompanied by Tony, she would have no choice but to smile sweetly and to pretend that she likes him. She knew that Tony is a no-nonsense person.

Aunt B was sitting at the diningtable with Tony and me. Suddenly a broad grin came over her face, stretching her mouth from ear to ear! She could hardly wait to voice her opinion. "Mass Tony," she exclaimed, "That's what me like with you. You don't put up with foolishness! I told G today that she must not worry about what people think about you. It is her life and furthermore, is not them bring her into this world; her mother dead and gone."

Tony thinks the world of Aunt B. The fact that she acts more like a mother to us, and has such words of wisdom, she can't do anything wrong in his eyes. Those words from Aunt B, was right up Tony's street." He was already a big head, but at that moment, I am sure that there was not a hat in the entire world which would fit his head.

He looked across the table at Aunt B, "Would you like to come along?" he asked.

"No, Mass Tony, me don't want to have any argument with Eth for I would just tell her that G is of age, she is not G's mother, and that as far as I am concerned, you are one hundred times more of a man than Claude. We know that she still worships the ground that Claude walks on. She love Claude because him have high colour (a very light complexion, almost half white), and because Claude have pretty hair [straight hair]."

Conversation closed, I went off to get myself ready for what I thought would be the confrontation of my life!

After a short brisk walk, Tony and I arrived at my sister's apartment. I stepped in front of Tony to smooth the way. "Good evening, Eth," I said in a kind of semi-nervous voice.

Without returning my greeting, she looked straight over my shoulder and straight through Tony!

"Mass Tony, what breeze blow you here now?" she remarked. "I hope is good breeze." Tony chuckled in his usual robust voice. Almost instantly she changed her greeting pattern, to one of respect and courtesy. "Come into me little humble apartment, me place no nice like yours, but me sure you can find a chair to sit down," she said to Tony. "Well, what have I done to deserve this visit from you?" she continued, "What has G been telling you about me?"

"Nothing, replied Tony, "but I am here to tell you something about G and myself. We are going to get married!" Well I was pleasantly surprised at her reaction. I expected a cold reception, but instead there was an atmosphere of excitement. "What? When?" she exclaimed with a bright glow in her eyes. She jumped up from her chair, gave Tony a 'bear hug' that almost squeezed the air out of his lungs! "Congrats, and may I be the first to wish you both God's blessings." I could hardly believe my ears, or my eyes. For a moment I thought that I was hallucinating. It was then my turn for the 'bear hug'. "Well G, you know that I am your second mother, and I will do my best to act the part.

She then sprang up from her chair and opened the door of her sideboard. "Well, I am not a drinker, but Papa (Father) would say, this call for a drink of white rum. I don't have white rum, but I have some ruby wine. She put out three glasses, opened the bottle of wine, and poured. "Raise your glasses," she said, with her usual broad smile. "Well here's to my future brother-in-law, or should I say the groom-to-be, and my dear sister, the bride-to-be." She took a sip of wine and swallowed. "Well, no more Mass Tony for me. From now on its Tony and G." I have never seen my sister so happy, except once when she won a lot of money at the horse races.

"Now we must tell the rest of the family, especially those in the country, to give them enough time to make plans." I sat with amazement, wine glass in hand, as I listened to my sister making my wedding plans. "I want you to get married in the cathedral, I want a big wedding. I don't want any of them little small churches to marry you." She then went on to choose the best-man, a middle-aged, middle-class gentleman. "We want four bridesmaids, and one page-boy. I will be chief bridesmaid. We want at least a three-tier cake. Miss Patsy is a very good cake-maker. I was quite elated by the whole experience. I said to myself, "it is no wonder the Bible says in St. Matthew, chapter 7, verse 1, 'Judge not, that ye be not judged'" My sister was truly 'a sheep in wolfes clothing.' During the rest of the evening, she could talk about nothing except my wedding!

When it was time to say goodbye, I was almost happy to leave. I had heard so much talk about the wedding, that I was glad to give it a break.

During the following weeks, the wedding plans really took off. A guest list was drawn up, invitation cards were printed, wedding cake was ordered, both male and female cooks were contacted, families who lived in the country areas were informed. One of my brothers who lived in the country, a well-established farmer, was asked to supply chickens, goats, one pig and lots of ground foods. The best-man, bridesmaids and page-boy were contacted. Materials for the bridesmaids' dresses were bought from a top store, and a high-class dressmaker was assigned to make the dresses. The best-man and page-boy suits were chosen and bought by

Tony. My wedding gown and accessories were bought ready-made from a top-class bridal gown departmental store.

The minister was also consulted. Tony and I attended several pre-wedding rehearsals. Suddenly the wedding plans were moving so fast, I could hardly keep up the pace! Families and friends were all in a state of "wedding fever".

Soon it was time to order bouquets for the chief-bridesmaid, bridesmaids, and my own bouquet. It was also time to make an appointment with my hairdresser and also with the beautician. Before I could count to ten, the great day had arrived!

The night before the wedding, Tony slept at his aunt's. It was a belief that if the bride and groom to be slept in the same house the night before the wedding, the marriage would be dogged by bad luck. I woke up on the morning of my wedding to find that I could not stop my knees from shaking. I was terrified!

I managed to have some breakfast, and then it was off to the hairdresser. I sat in the hairdresser's chair for what seemed like hours. Finally, she finished grooming and styling my hair; she apologised nicely and gave the reason for taking so long as having to style the hair so that the tiara sat perfectly. When I looked in the mirror I could hardly believe my eyes. I had never seen a hair-do so beautiful. I felt just like a film star!

I then went off to have my facial. I can still feel the very hot towels on my face, followed by ice-cold water, followed by what seemed like gallons of creams! At the end of it all, I could hardly recognize myself. I looked just like a princess. Suddenly my knees stopped shaking, as I imagined myself as the most beautiful young bride of the year!

After my facial, I walked the short distance from the beauty salon to my apartment. I arrived to find that Aunt B had cooked me a lovely lunch. There was only one problem, I had lost my appetite. After some coaxing from Aunt B, I managed to eat a small portion of what she called my bridal lunch. Before long, it was time to get dressed for my big moment. I was helped by the chief-bridesmaid, my very own senior sister. She was just like a mother to me. She fussed, and fussed, and made quite sure that every hair was in place. Finally, the drama came to an end. My bridal gown was white with lace bodice, which had a low-cut neckline, long sleeves with pointed cuffs. The waist of the bodice fitted tightly in what was called an A-line. The skirt was ankle-length, made up with yards of lace, and lined with a very stiff lining, which looked almost as wide as a tent!

My hair was adorned with a shoulder-length veil, attached to a skull hat, covered with pearls. These were complimented with a pearl necklace, earrings, white lace gloves, and satin white bridal shoes. I carried a beautiful bouquet of white lilies.

Finally, the bridal car arrived. My chief-bridesmaid helped me into the car. I sat in the back seat feeling rather nervous, which was an understatement. As the car drove off, I was simply terrified. I could hardly believe that in a few minutes I would be married!

As this all happened on a sunny Saturday afternoon, there were crowds of people on every street. People opened their windows and waved as the car went by. When I arrived at the cathedral, the crowd was so thick I could hardly get through. That was when I really felt my knees shaking. People were cheering and shouting congratulations. Some should out, "Good luck, Mass Tony," some shouted, "God bless you both." Others shouted aloud, "You look nice, Miss G."

As I entered the cathedral, I could see Tony standing at the top of the isles, hands clasped in front and a smile that said, "You look lovely, my darling."

As I looked around the cathedral, I could hardly believe my eyes. There was not one vacant seat to be found. It all seemed like a beautiful dream, and I began to wonder if I would wake up to find that all of this was not real!

I continued walking slowly down the aisle, surrounded by the chief-bridesmaid, bridesmaids and page-boy, to the tune of 'Here comes the Bride', which was being played on the huge pipe organ. Suddenly the tears started to run down my cheeks. Tried as I could, I could not stop the tears from falling. The emotion was just too great to contain. At that moment I knew what it was like to cry tears of joy.

After walking for what seemed like the length of a cricket pitch, I found myself standing beside my husband-to-be. Tony glanced at me lovingly, and smiled the sweetest smile ever. As I glanced at him, I smiled back. That was when the chief-bridesmaid noticed that I was crying. She produced a white lace handkerchief and wiped away the tears from my eyes.

The minister started the wedding ceremony, and for the very first time I saw signs of nervousness in Tony's voice. He could hardly repeat the wedding vows. His voice choked with emotion, as he fought back the tears which had welled up in his eyes. Being the tough type of guy that he was, he managed to complete the wedding vows without one single tear falling down his cheek. I looked in his eyes and thought, that's just like Tony.

It was now my turn to repeat my wedding vows, when the flood gates opened and rivers of water just poured down my face. Once again, the chief bridesmaid came to the rescue by producing the magical white lace handkerchief with which she gently mopped up the tears. As I prayed silently, *Dear God please help me stop crying*, the tears immediately dried up, and I managed to complete my marriage vows.

As the minister took the wedding rings from the small white heart-shaped lace pillow, which was held by the page-boy, and began to bless them, I felt my own heart beating so loud, the beats were almost audible. I knew then that I really loved Tony with all of my heart. After Tony had repeated the lines, "With this ring, I thee wed," followed by the rest of the wedding vows, he lovingly placed the ring on my wedding finger.

The minister then said, "I now pronounce you, husband and wife." He then turned to Tony and said, "You may now kiss the bride." As Tony lifted the veil from my face to kiss me, I felt quite embarrassed. Although I was now a married woman, that sense of respect for my elders was still there, and I could hardly bring myself to kiss Tony in front of my elder sister, and other senior men and women.

The wedding vows now completed, my entourage, the minister and I went off to the large office situated at the back of the cathedral for the signing of the register. As I held the gold fountain pen which belonged to the minister in my hand, my hand started trembling. It was quite a battle to control the now visible shaking of my hand. Again, I whispered a silent prayer, *Dear God, please stop my hand from shaking*. Again God answered my prayer. Almost immediately the vigorous shaking stopped. As I signed, the cameraman flashed a blinding light with his camera as he took a photograph of the grand occasion.

This part of the ceremony completed, the procession slowly walked out of the minister's office, and down the aisle toward the front door of the cathedral. The organist played a most beautiful tune as my new husband, myself and the best-man, chief-bridesmaid, bridesmaids and page-boy slowly walked down the aisle. As I stepped out of the front door, I was showered with confetti and white rice. The white rice was thrown by an old lady, who believed that white rice thrown over the bride was a sign of good luck. Then came loud shouts of, "Good luck," and, "God bless you both, may you two live like rice and peas."

As I was helped into the bridal car, I could still hear the joyful shouts of old and young people alike. It was one of the happiest moments of my life! As the car sped off, I wound down the window and waved to the happy crowd. As we drove along the crowded streets to the reception, it was a repeat of the way it was when we drove along to the cathedral. People selling stuffs on the sidewalk, waved and shouted their congratulations. People on the way to the market, people coming from the market all added their voices to shout their congratulations! It was like a scene from *Seven brides for Seven Brothers*.

Finally, the bridal car followed by many others, arrived at the reception. I had another surprise awaiting me. The crowd gathered from the entrance of the street to a good distance beyond the entrance gate to the reception. I was met by a barrage of shouts and cheers, as I struggled through the sea of happy faces, to push my way into the reception hall. I must honestly say I was not prepared for anything like this!

After the usual formalities, a hush came over the entire hall, as Tony and I rose from our seats, to take the floor for our first dance as man and wife. As he took me into his arms, and held me so tight, yet so gentle, we waltzed to the tune, 'I can't Stop Loving You' by Ray Charles. As we waltzed around the hall, at times not moving, just swaying our bodies, as Tony gazed lovingly into my eyes, I felt as though this was just a dream, and that very soon I would wake up into reality! As the record continued to play until the end, and I did not wake up, I realized that this was not a dream, this was for real!

At what I thought was the end of the waltz, I was making my way to sit down, when the crowd shouted, "Encore," several times! They all remained seated, and continued to shout, "Encore!" They wanted to see Tony and I dance once more. I must confess I was not a bit sorry. I secretly wished that we could stay locked into each other's arms and dance all night. We returned to the centre of the floor, and the waltz, much to the satisfaction of the crowd. They clapped and whistled, and cheered, from the beginning to the end of the record!

At the end of the waltz, the crowd all joined in to dance to the lovely sixties records. Even now, as I am putting this on paper, I can see in my mind's eye the happy occasion. It is something that I cannot erase from my memory. At one point, the merry-making was turned into a twisting contest, as they twisted to the tune, "Let's Twist Again", by Chubby Checker. Everyone wanted to prove that they were the best "twister". Everyone was doing the "twist", regardless of age. I would not be surprised if some folks did not do themselves an injury, but decided to grin and bear the pain, as they wanted to win the contest so badly!

After the "twist", it was time for the boogie, and the calypso! By this time, Tony and I had gone home and changed out of our wedding attire. I now felt free to dance without tripping up over my wedding gown. Now I could really let my hair down! There was just one element of unhappiness which occurred at the end of the merry-making. I found out that someone had stolen my beautiful white lace table-cloth. Although I was very upset, I refused to let it spoil my big day. It could be that the person thought that, if they took something that they could keep, some of the happiness of the day would rub off on them.

The next day after the wedding, being Sunday, and as customary Tony and I went to worship at the cathedral where we were married. Only this time I was not nervous. I felt a sense of boldness, as we were escorted to the front pew to be seated. Although it was a lovely service, I did not enjoy it the way I should have, as I was still very exhausted. As a matter of fact, I was glad when the service came to an end. We returned home to a beautiful Sunday dinner, lovingly prepared by Aunt B. After dinner, it was time to start packing to go away on our honeymoon. The following morning we were up very early, before the sun got too hot, to set out on the long drive to a remote village to spend our honeymoon with Tony's father and his step-mother. I was very apprehensive, but felt at ease somewhat, as we drove up the hill, on a small dirt track, past a small village school, Tony exclaimed, "That is where I went to school." A short distance after we passed a small grocery store, "That is where I used to come as a small boy to buy the groceries," he said.

Soon he stopped outside a small wooden house, which nestled amongst some orange and grapefruit trees. "We are home," he exclaimed, with a broad grin on his face. We got out of the car and were greeted by a lovely big brown dog. He didn't appear too friendly, as he came rushing towards the car snarling and barking. I rushed back into the car and shut the door. "Come Pup-pups," Tony calmly said to the dog. With that greeting, Pup-pups jumped up at Tony and they began to play. "Open the car door" "Tony" said to me, in a very calm voice. "He won't hurt you."

I was still very reluctant to open the car door. Then before I could answer Tony, a very pretty middle-aged, light-skinned lady with shoulder-length black hair wearing a broad smile, strolled towards the car. She opened the car door. "Hello Gloria," she said. She then ordered the dog to go in. Pup-pups, wagged his tail and walked away towards the house. Only then would I come out of the car. She gave me a big hug, which made me feel welcome and at ease.

After spending one week with my new in-laws, we returned home. My first few days of married life were absolute bliss. I felt so very proud of myself. In those days, it was seen as being very lucky to get married at an early age. One was well respected by young and old. That was the only time when the boot was on the other foot. Usually it's the young who show respect for the old, but if it is a case where the young person is married, the old show them great respect. Suddenly I was referred to as 'Mrs. H' by young and old alike. Tony was so proud of his new status; he would continually refer to me as 'his wife'. As far as Tony was concerned, I had lost my name. To him I had become "his wife". I hasten to add, the wife with no name. His friends would say to me, "Why does your husband always refer to you as my wife, my wife, my wife?" Have you lost your name?' I would feel quite embarrassed, although I would try not to show my embarrassment by putting on a brave smile.

Not very long after we got married, the 'going to England craze' began. Almost all our best friends were going to England. I could not understand the reason why, as most of them had very good jobs. Some were teachers, some were Accountants, and some worked in the banks, record office, and so on. Then suddenly, I caught the England "fever," after my best friend, who was like a sister to me, left for England. I told Tony I wanted to go to England. At first he was surprised, then after giving the matter some thought, he said, "If that is what you want, and if it makes you happy, you can go. I will stay behind, and if you don't like it, you can come back home."

At that time there was a recruitment programme going on for nurse training in England. From a very young age, I had always wanted to be a nurse, and thought this was the ideal opportunity to do so. I went into town, took the test for nurse training in the U.K, and passed with flying colours. I was very happy, when the lady who was conducting the tests, told me that I had passed. I went home from the recruitment centre with a tinge of both happiness and sadness. Happiness because I had always wanted to travel to the U.K, Canada or America, and now was my chance to go to the U.K. Sadness, because I was very much in love with my darling husband Tony, and deep down inside of me, I really did not want to go away without him. I suddenly found myself in a great dilemma. One half of me wanted to go to the U.K, and the other half of me wanted to stay with Tony. *Help* I thought, *now what do I do?*

I knew I had to come to a decision, however painful the decision might be. Finally, I decided to go to the U.K. I told my senior sister who brought me up, also the rest of the family about my intended travel plans. I was very surprised to find that not one single person in my very large family was enthusiastic about my plans! It was very clear to see that I was on my own. Again, I reverted back to a period of very deep contemplation. The more I thought about the matter, the clearer it became that there was no way Tony could afford to pay the fees for me to enter nurse training to enable me to fulfil my life's ambition.

The airfare to the UK was £85 which, in those days, was a lot of money! Most people travelled by boat which was cheaper at £75. I decided that I would not travel by boat because, apart from the fact that I don't like boats, my main reason being that I cannot swim, and I always had this fear that, if God forbid something should go wrong and I have to swim to save my life, I certainly could not do it. Furthermore, I had heard several horror stories about people who travelled to the U.K. by boat.

My next move was to apply to hospitals in the U.K. asking them to be accepted for the post of trainee nurse. At the same time I wrote to a friend who had not long settled in the U.K. to ask if she would be willing to accommodate me for a short period on my arrival in the U.K. until I found my own accommodation. My travel now depended on those two parties. I need not have worried. It was not long after my applications to the various hospitals, that I had welcoming replies from all the hospitals that I had applied to. One particular hospital sounded as though they really could not wait to have me! I put the quick replies down to my girlish appearance, broad smile and short-cropped afro hair, which I had dyed dark brown! Needlessy to say, I was over joyed at the prompt replies. I was even offered living-in accommodation by all the hospitals. There and then I began to imagine myself in my white uniform, crisply starched apron, hat, white shoes and white socks. I could hardly contain myself. I forgot to add that I had to send a photograph of myself with all my applications.

It was now really a matter of waiting for a favourable reply from my girlfriend, whether or not she would be willing to accommodate me on my arrival.

It was not long before I received a reply from my friend with regards to my intended travel to the U.K., and my dependence on her for short-term accommodation. On the morning that the letter arrived, I was very apprehensive as to the contents. I finally opened the letter with somewhat trembling hands, and racing pulse! I was pleasantly surprised to find that she was more than willing to accommodate me. She went on to describe London in as much detail as she could. It sounded quite good, but there was no mention of "the streets paved with gold" as we were made to believe. After turning over the mental picture of London in my mind, I felt sure that I could settle there.

During the course of that day, I picked the letter up and read it over and over, and over again, and again, and again. I can't remember how many times I read that letter that day! At the back of my mind I kept wondering if I had made the right decision. When Tony returned home from work that evening, I could hardly wait to tell him about the letter, and to get him to read the contents. I sat nervously at the dinner table, wondering whether or not he would change his mind about my going to the U.K. After what seemed like sitting at the dining table for hours, the meal finally came to an end, and it was time to tell Tony that I had a reply from my friend, and gave him the letter. I sat nervously at the table waiting for Tony's reply. He had that look on his face that said, *well that's not what I want, but if that is what you want, I won't stand in your way.* "Well," he replied, "Now that you have decided to go, we will have a lot of sorting out to do. There is the matter of how we are going to raise the fare; we will also have to make sure that "Aunt B" stays with me to look after me while you are away, and so on."

During that week, I went into town to see the travel agent about making my travel plans. It was as though that wonderful Chinese gentleman could read my mind! Before I could say one word, he said, "You don't have to pay all the money at once. You can make a small deposit, and pay the rest when and how you can!" Those words were like music to my ears. *Thank you Jesus*, I said within myself. Then I replied, "thank you sir." He then gave me a list of available flight dates, and flight times. I had an option of travelling in the summer months, or the winter months. It would have given me more time to pay off the balance if I had chosen the winter months, but I really did not want to be landing in the U.K. in the winter if I could avoid doing so. I therefore chose to travel in June.

After making a small deposit, I was given a receipt for the money which I had paid. The feel of that receipt in the palm of my hands was to me as precious as the feel of £1,000,000! I checked it several times, not to see if it was right, but to make sure that it was actually a receipt for the deposit on my airfare to the U.K. After I had convinced myself that it was what it was, I folded it with great respect and put it away safely in my handbag. I then proceeded to depart from that office with a spring in my step, as though I was walking on air! On my way to the bus stop, the thought kept turning over in my mind, I have done it! I have actually booked my fare to the U.K. I could sense the glow on my face. I was sure that everyone who glanced at my face could see that I was extremely happy. Finally, I got to the bus stop and, after what seemed like a very lengthy wait, the bus came. I boarded the bus, still with that glow on my face. I sat down in an empty seat, on the left-hand side of the bus. I was in a world of my own. I did not hear the bus-conductor shout for my fare. I was sitting on the bus, but my mind was in the U.K. I was thinking of those streets paved with gold, covered over in the winter months, with thick snow! Suddenly there was an almighty poke in my side with fingers which felt like a sledgehammer, followed by a voice which sounded like thunder, "You nah pay you fare, missis? wha happen? you in a dream lan'?" [Aren't you going to pay your fare? What has happened? Are you in dreamland?]" I quickly apologised and hurriedly opened my purse and paid my fare before the already angry and hostile conductor got the impression that I was fare dodging! He snatched the money from my hands. "You better wake up," he replied. "What happen? The sun hat drunk you? [Is the sun so hot that it makes you drunk?]"

After a very lengthy ride in a very hot and extremely over-crowded bus, which made me feel as though I was shut up in an oven, rather like the Sunday roast, I alighted to walk the short distance home. I was tooted by car drivers several times as I crossed the busy streets, still in dreamland. One angry car driver shouted from his wound down car window "Wa rong wid you, gal? You wa get run ober? [What is wrong with you girl? do you want to get run-over?]" At that point, I gave myself a slap on the wrist, and told myself, *Come on, pull yourself together, or you might just walk "the streets of gold" that you were told about in Sunday school.* With that possibility almost becoming a reality several times during my short walk, I snapped out of my dream walking.

Finally, by the grace of God, I managed to arrive home safely. I breathed a great sigh of relief, and whispered the words, "Thank God," and sat down in my favourite veranda chair, closed my eyes, and just allowed the gentle breeze to cool me down. In that relaxed frame of mind, I just could not stop my imagination running off to the U.K. I started to imagine the people, the houses; me working on the wards, me sitting by the coal-fire during the winter months, seeing myself dressed up in winter coats, boots, scarf, gloves, etc. I even saw myself eating fish and chips from newspaper. All the things that my girlfriend wrote and told me about in her recent letter were coming alive in my imagination. Eventually, after some time had elapsed, I woke up from the imaginary state of mind, and found myself still sitting in my armchair! I smiled sweetly, and went inside to change my clothes. I locked my treasured receipt in my jewel box, and tried to settle down to a snack.

After I had deflated my imaginary balloon, I sat down to have a chat with Aunt B. Although she was somewhat pleased for me, I could sense a tinge of sadness in her voice. Her usual cheerful countenance was also absent. Pretending not to notice her sadness, I forced a smile, and she managed to smile back at me, but I could see that her smile was lacking reality. As I took a closer look into her eyes, I could see the tears welling up in her eyes. At that point I broke the conversation and said, "Aunt B, how about a large cool glass of sour sap juice?" I deliberately asked for sour sap juice, because I knew that it would take a long time to prepare, thus giving her time to pull herself together.

When she returned with the prepared juice, I started the conversation by saying, "Don't worry, if I don't like it in the U.K., I will return home."

I could almost hear her say in her heart, "I hope when you go there, you don't like it, and you come home."

I managed to continue the dialogue with great strain as I tried very hard to hide my emotions. Finally, it came to a point where I had to give her instructions how to carry on her duties in my absence. Again, I could see that she was almost in tears. I reminded her of my previous statement, that if I did not like it in the U.K., I would return home. On the sound of those words falling on her ears, she conjured up a brave smile, and I felt the confidence to carry on the conversation. It was the most difficult dialogue I had ever had with Aunt B. I remember finishing the conversation, with the words, "If you have any problems don't be afraid to write and tell me." On those re-assuring notes, the conversation came to an end.

The next few months were crucial. It was a time when my brains and Tony's worked overtime to think of ways and means, how to go about getting the £85 to pay my airfare to the U.K. As I have said earlier, in those days £85 was a lot of money! We must have spent hours talking about the subject of 'money finding'. Finally, I decided to swallow my pride, and took the long, hot, rough, over-crowded bus ride down to the country, to one of my elder brothers who was an established farmer, to ask him to lend me some money to help me with paying my fare. I assured him that as soon as I started working, I would pay him the money back. I felt as though the stuffing was knocked out of me when he said, "Sorry, G I can't help you, a done hav any money. [Sorry, I am unable to help you, I don't have any money]." I almost burst into tears. I felt so very sure that he would be able to help me, because I knew that he had money. "Well," I said to myself, "I know that God will provide," one of my mother's favourite quotations. Whenever she had a need, and humans could not, or would not help her, she would breathe a huge sigh and say, "God will provide," and those words worked like magic. God would always provide!

With those comforting words taken from the text book of my mother, I managed to stay composed the rest of the day, and chatted cheerfully with his dear wife as he went off to the field to do his farming, and attend to his many cows. After taking in some fresh unpolluted country air, sitting on the well-furnished veranda, and strolling around the well-fruited yard, it was time for lunch. Lunch was a very heavy meal of cooked yams, green bananas, sweet potatoes and dumplings, accompanied by freshly caught fish. That was the custom of the country folks. After lunch, I just helped myself to grapefruits, oranges, mandarins etc., which was plentiful around the house; enough fruits and ground provisions to last me for a very long time. Living in the town, this was just magic!

I packed a large bag with the freshly picked fruits, green bananas, breadfruits, and freshly dug yams, sweet potatoes, and dasheen. These items are very expensive in the towns. After so doing, with my very badly dented ego, I managed to keep smiling, almost fighting back the tears. I went to the bathroom, had a wash and powdered my face in readiness for my very long uncomfortable journey on the cramped country bus, which would take me back home to town in a travelling time of approximately four hours! Needless-to-say, I was not looking forward to my return journey. On reaching my destination, Tony was waiting for me. Thank God he drove the car to collect me, and I did not have to walk the short journey home. I really didn't think I could have made it.

As soon as I got in the car, his very first words were, "Did you get the money?" I felt as though someone had poured concrete down my throat as I tried to muster up the courage to force the two-letter word 'NO' out from my voice box! "What!" He exclaimed, "You mean to tell me that your brother wid so much money coulden' lend you a smalls? [You are telling me that your brother, who has so much money, could not lend you a small part of your fare?]" I felt really quite ashamed as I was always boasting to Tony about my rich brother who lived in the country, who had a very large farm, lots of cows, battery farmed chickens, and that he supplied many of the large hotels in town with chickens and eggs. "Well," he replied, in his husky voice, "What is that saying your mother had?"

"God will provide," I replied.

When we got home and I had my town supper lovingly prepared by my dear Aunt B, Tony and I settled down on the veranda, in our comfortable veranda chairs, and yes, you got it in one, up cropped the raising-of-the-money head. At this point, I began to feel quite irritable, and almost lost my cool as I said in an almost shouting tone of voice, "Don't worry, please change the subject, God will make a way, when it seems that there is no way." With this statement, spoken in a somewhat sharp tone of voice, Tony got the message and changed the conversation.

As we sat in deep contemplation about how we were going to raise the required amount of the outstanding balance of my airfare, I suddenly had a brain wave. *Why not sell some of the furniture?* I thought. The house was very well furnished, and I was certain that I would like it in the U.K., therefore, in the not too distant future Tony would join me, and he would then have to sell off all or most of the furniture. "Tony," I said "Why don't we sell some of the furniture to help us find the rest of the money to pay my fare?" He thought for a moment then he replied, "That's a very good idea. I am almost sure that you will like it in the U.K., and that I will join you soon, at least in three months' time. I would then have to sell off the furniture. They are almost new and, therefore, people will be glad to buy them."

On that note we drew up a list of the things that we would dispose of. The double bed would go, complete with my beautiful panelled headboard with painted basket of flowers, the cooker would go and would be replaced with a smaller one, the ironing-board would also be sold, and Aunt B would have to manage by doing the ironing on the table. That would not be a problem. She did the ironing that way before I was able to buy the ironingboard.

Word went around by word of mouth, which was quicker than a telephone, to say we were selling certain items of furnishing. Before long, people came around to the house in droves to buy the items. There was one problem; they all wanted the items on credit. Some people said they would pay next week, some in the next two weeks, some at the end of the month, and some had no specific time when they would pay. They would only say, "Me wi pay you soon, Miss G [I will pay you as soon as I can "Miss G]". Although they appeared sincere in their offer, that was not what I wanted. I needed cash on delivery, as I wanted to finish paying the remaining balance on my fare as soon as possible. I was in a dilemma. *What shall I do?* I asked myself. Do I take the risk and give these people the furniture on credit, and hope that they would pay at the time specified? Or do I try to find another way out. I thought on the matter for a very long time, and could not find any other option! With somewhat very heavy heart I decided to let them have the items after paying a small deposit. Now I can only hope and pray that they would keep their word and not disappoint me!

Unfortunately, I had a very difficult time collecting the outstanding balance on the items sold. There was this well-to-do woman, who credited my cooker. She lived just around the corner from where I lived. It was a very frustrating situation trying to collect the money she owed on the cooker. Each time I called, I was told that she was not at home. I got the same reply each time I called, be it morning, noon or night. The thing which I feared most was happening. I had a niggling fear at the back of my mind, that this particular woman would do her very best to avoid paying, knowing full well that I had to leave for the U.K. fairly soon. That was exactly what happened. She never paid me one penny, except for the small deposit which she made initially. My husband wrote to me in the U.K. to say, he had tried on several occasions to collect the remaining balance of money from this woman, but without success.

By the grace of God, I managed to pay off the remaining balance of my airfare on a "pay as you can" basis, after making several trips into town on the much over-crowded town bus. I hated every minute of the journey, which I frequently took, to and from town. I will never forget the day that I made my final payment. The only time I felt that happy was on my wedding day. I can almost hear the words of Mr. Chen ringing in my ears. "Well," he said, "this is your last payment." He then reached for his receipt book, and wrote me out my final receipt. "Thank God," I replied, throwing up my hands in the air. He smiled sweetly, shook my hands, wished me a safe flight to the U.K., and said goodbye. On that happy note, I opened the door, let myself out with the happy knowledge that this was to be my last visit.

A few days later, I returned to town, to buy my suitcase, and the outfit that I would travel in to the U.K. The fact that I haven't travelled abroad before, I had no idea of the type of suitcase to buy. My eyes caught this beautiful large suitcase, red and grey in colour. *That's the one* I thought to myself. I will buy that one, forgetting that I was only allowed forty-four pounds in weight, and also forgetting to feel the weight of the suitcase, I just went ahead and bought it. Although it felt a bit heavy as I walked along the busy streets, I still did not think that it was too heavy! I soon realised the weight, as I tried to carry it in and out of the busy stores, shopping for my dress and matching accessories. As I struggled in and out of the crowded stores, people looked at me, and then they glanced down at the very large suitcase as if to say, where is she going with that? The joy, with which I had left the travel service, suddenly began to fade, as I soon realised that I was becoming a laughing stock! I managed to put on a brave face, and carried on shopping regardless. I must admit that it was a very difficult performance. At one point, one man shouted out of his car window, "High missus, a wey you a go wid that deh house? [Where are you going with that suitcase it is as big as a house?]" I was almost in tears, but God was on my side. In the very next shop, which was an exclusive shop for the rich and famous, I decided to pluck up the courage and venture inside. The shop assistant looked down at the suitcase before she looked at my face. Then she looked up at me somewhat surprised! "Can I help you?" she said.

"Yes," I replied. "I am looking for a peach suit and matching hat, shoes and gloves."

She looked somewhat puzzled, "Suit hat and gloves?" she repeated.

"Yes," I said, "Suit, hat and gloves."

"Where are you going with suit, hat and gloves?" she remarked.

"England," I said. She took me to the clothing department and, as I entered, my eyes caught the very kind of suit that I had in mind. A beautiful cream dress, which featured a fine pleated skirt, and jacket with long sleeves. I tried it on and it fitted like a glove. I was over the moon with joy! I also found a hat, shoes, gloves and handbag, all in the same shop. Looking back now, I realise that God had led me to that store, which under normal circumstances I would not have gone to. He did this to prevent me having to endure further embarrassment! I whispered a silent thank you prayer to God, paid my bill and left the shop.

Unfortunately, that was not the end of my large suitcase problem! From the time I walked out of that shop, people began looking at my suitcase and laughing. If more than one person was walking together they would look, whisper and sometimes just burst out laughing. My now shaking knees were under great stress to take me to the bus stop which was quite a long walk away, and I had to walk along very a very crowded sidewalk. I could not avoid bumping into people. They would turn around and shout "Gal, mine me wid you big ole grip [Girl, look where you are going, and don't bump into me with that large suitcase]." I had no choice but to endure that unkind abuse all the way to the bus stop.

Waiting for that bus was like waiting for Christmas! It seemed as though it was taking ages to arrive, although in reality, I did not wait that long. I was very much aware of the look, stares, whispers and laughter, as I stood at the bus stop. Finally, the bus arrived. I had great difficulty pushing my way through the free-for-all disorderly crowd onto the bus. One woman shouted, "Look ya gal move out a de way, mek people get pan de bus [Look here girl move out of the way so that people can get on the bus]." Eventually I made it onto the crowded bus. I sat down beside the woman. As I struggled to make myself comfortable with the suitcase on my lap, she looked at me and just burst out laughing! This drew the attention of the entire bus load of passengers, including the driver and the bus conductor. Everyone started laughing. I was the only one who was not laughing, as I did not think it was funny! The bus conductor walked down from the front of the bus towards the middle of the bus where I was sitting, took a good look at my suitcase and burst into laughter, so much so that the tears began to run down his face. He suddenly stopped laughing and exclaimed, "A England you a go, boy me ha fi charge you two fair, one fi you, an one fi the house. [Are you going to England? I will have to charge you two fares, one for you and one for your large suitcase]." Again he roared out in laughter, followed by the passengers and bus driver. He then walked back to the front of the bus, and started collecting the fares. As soon as he got to where I was sitting, he roared out laughing, stretched his hand out to me and joked, "A two fair me a charge you, you know. [I am charging you two fares]." I gave him my fare and tried to keep my composure. Needless-to-say, they all giggled all the way, until I alighted from the bus.

After alighting from the bus, I had to walk about half a mile to where I lived. Of course, the large suitcase talk began all over again. As I passed people who knew that I was travelling to the U.K. shortly, they would stop me, look at the suitcase, and would actually say to me, "Miss G," don't you think this suitcase is too big?" The people that I did not know, such as the country folks who would come to my town, to sell their produce, sitting on the sidewalk, they would have a good look, and just grin!

That evening, when Tony came home from work, as soon as he saw the suitcase, he picked it up, weighed it by just holding it in his hands, and feeling the weight. Then he said, "G, this suitcase is much too heavy. Although it is empty it feels as though it weighs over forty pounds! How much will it weigh when it is packed?" Those words from Tony made me feel as though the bottom had just fallen out of my world. "Well," I said, "I am certainly not taking it back to town to change it for a smaller one." I did not tell Tony the real reason why I did not want to take back the suitcase. He would only say, "Don't worry about what people say." Tony is that type of a person. "What are you going to do?" he said. "How are you going to take the things that you need to take, if you won't take the suitcase back and exchange it?" I felt rather silly, as I gave him the following reply. "I will leave them, and you can post them to me." He looked a bit surprised. "Post them?" he replied, isn't it easier to take the suitcase back, and change it for a smaller one?"

"I am not going back to town," I said. "The bus is too crowded and hot."

During the next few days I was extremely busy sorting out the necessary things that I needed for my journey to the U.K. Needless to say I could not pack half the items! No sooner than I had put in a few things, the suitcase felt as though it weighed one hundred pounds. I was in a state of bewilderment. I decided to pack only the things that I really needed, and try to pack as much as possible in my hand luggage, but with all of that, I realised that I had to leave a lot of the things I needed to take behind. I gave a lot of my clothing and foot wear to Aunt B and other members of the family. I hasten to add that as far as they were concerned that was a blessing in disguise.

My next priority was to send a cable off to my friend in the U.K. to inform her of the date, flight number and expected time of my arrival in the U.K. After I did that, the "have I done the right thing" thought kept coming into my mind! *Well*, I told myself, *it is too late now to change my mind. I am going to the U.K. and that's final!* Each time I looked at the packed suitcase and hand luggage, complete with label, a tear fell from my eyes. The reality of it all was reinforced when I glanced at my well-pressed suit hanging outside my wardrobe, large brown felt hat, accompanied by shoes and gloves nearby. This time, not only a tear fell from my eyes, but a river of tears ran down my cheeks, followed by a vigorous shaking of the knees; at this point all the what-ifs in the world kept coming in my mind. What if I don't like the U.K., what if no one comes to meet me? To name but two out of a thousand.

The day before the big day, Tony kept telling me how much he loved me, and how much he will miss me. He then went on to say, "I don't know how I will manage without you." Well that almost made me crack up. That night, neither of us slept for more than five minute intervals. We kissed and cuddled, and chatted all night. The following morning we were up at the break of dawn. Aunt B arrived at the house very early. She looked extremely sad. She hardly spoke as she made herself busy preparing what she called, my 'farewell breakfast'. I had my early morning cold shower, ate breakfast, with great difficulty, as I tried to hold back the tears. Breakfast finished, it was time to get ready for the fairly lengthy drive to the airport. I was accompanied by Aunt B, other family members, and my very best girlfriend, who was more like a sister than a friend. On the way to the airport, Tony, along with everyone else, tried very hard to keep a cheerful conversation going. As we drove along the road, I took a long hard look at everything that I passed, as if to say, "Well, I don't know when I will see you again!" It was a very strange feeling, one that I can't really explain. One picture stuck in my mind the most. As we went over a certain bridge, under which a very special river flowed, it brought back to memory the days when Tony and I used to go to a certain spot along the bank of that river and just hold hands and chat as we used to watch the crayfish glide along downstream. I still have, in my sixties photo album, a very special photograph which I took sitting on the trunk of a tree which had up-rooted and fell into that river. Although this photograph is in black and white, I would not part with it for all the money in the world. It means so much to me!

At the end of the drive, which seemed more of a dream than reality, I woke up to the husky voice of Tony saying, "Well we are here." As I stepped out of the car, and my relatives unloaded my huge suitcase, and handluggage, I prayed silently, "Dear God, please don't let me be over-weight!" At that very emotional point in time, I realised that this was truly the point of no return, and I was not completely sure that I was really prepared for it! Being a very busy airport, which was miles away from the folks who lived in the country, passengers and drivers, became very hostile and aggressive. Their aggression was made worse by the heat of the sun. They were always ready to toot you out of the way if you appeared to be moving too slowly. It was not long before one angry driver shouted, "Come on woman, yo tink me ha all day fi wait pon you. [Come on woman, do you think that I have all day to wait on you? Get moving.]" With that blast of insult, we hurried into the airport building and headed towards the check-in counter.

My knees got weaker, and weaker, with each step I took towards the check-in counter. At one stage, my feet decided to join rank with my knees, and decided to stick to the concrete flooring! It seemed as though I was using up a lot of energy as I dragged myself towards the check-in counter. Suddenly my tummy joined in as well! I felt butterflies invading my tummy, followed by a feeling of weakness, which almost made me crumble to the floor. At that point my emotions, which I had fought so long and so hard to keep, gave way, and I just burst out crying. Tony quickly and affectionately put his arms around me, and comforted me. My situation was made worse when the rest of the family, accompanied by my girlfriend, joined in the crying episode! Strangely enough, I felt that I was responsible for starting the crying chain; therefore, I felt I had to be the first to stop. This I managed to accomplish with great emotional difficulty, thus breaking the crying chain!

I was fortunate to have checked in early, thus giving me vital time before departure with Tony and family. These precious minutes seemed as though they went faster than the time it took to melt ice-cubes in the hot Caribbean sunshine! Before long my flight number was called. I held Tony in my arms and squeezed him so tightly I almost squeezed the air out of his lungs. This was followed by a loving, tender kiss. The most emotional kiss I had had from Tony since we met. Of course, this opened up the old wound of the crying saga all over again, and the tears just rolled down my cheeks; only this time I was unable to stop. As I tore myself away from Tony's arms, I felt a great emptiness and I suddenly felt quite alone. I was not sure how I could turn around, and took the first step away from Tony towards the required gate through which I had to go, which led to my now waiting aircraft. Trembling and visibly shaking, I walked away. As I walked along the fairly long gangway towards the aircraft, I must have looked back at Tony and the rest of friends and family one hundred times, or more! Finally, they vanished out of sight, and I was now really alone. As I ascended the flights of steps into the aircraft, I took one last long look, as though

by some miracle they would re-appear! Unfortunately, this
was not the case, and I stepped into the "Iron bird" which
was the name given to an aircraft by the natives. I was very
lucky to have been allocated a window seat.

Still shaking nervously, I nestled up close to the window.
Unable to accept reality I stared out of the somewhat dusty
aircraft window, still hoping against all odds to bless my tear
filled eyes on my beloved Tony, family and friends. Sadly,
this was an impossible wish which could not be granted.
Accepting defeat on this issue, I closed my eyes momentarily,
and went into deep meditation. The purpose of this action
was to see Tony in consciousness, as I had seen him a few
minutes ago! Fortunately, it worked. As I saw Tony smiling
sweetly at me I must have unconsciously brought a smile
to my face. Almost as though I was in a deep sleep, I was
awakened by a lady's voice saying, "Someone is very happy!"
At those words, I snapped out of my day-dreaming and
woke up to find that I was still on the ground, sitting at my
somewhat dusty aircraft window. Needless to say, I was not
a very happy young lady!

After a short while, a sign came up in lights, which read,
"Fasten your seat belt." This was followed by a man's voice
which said, "Ladies and gentlemen, welcome aboard flight
BA... bound for London Heathrow. In a moment you will
be shown some safety demonstrations. Please pay attention
as this exercise is very important." This was followed by a very
beautiful, smartly dressed airhostess who seemed to appear
from nowhere, in the aisle in front of where I was sitting.
She began by pointing out the escape routes which would be
used in case of an emergency. Then she demonstrated how
to put on the oxygen masks if they were needed. She also

demonstrated how to put on the life-jacket. It was all very frightening. I sat glued to my seat. I was physically shaking with fright! I wanted to shout, "Please stop, I want to get off," but could not.

After the demonstrations were completed, a final announcement was made. "Please make sure your seat is in the upright position, your tables in front of you are folded away, and your handbag etc. is under the seat in front of you." Then came the dreaded words, "Cabin crew, please take your seat for take-off!" At this point, I felt as though my heart had moved from my chest, and taken up position in my mouth. My pulse was beating so fast, I could count the beats without using a watch with a minute hand! Then came the roaring of the aircraft engines, and the feeling of movement. I looked out of the window, and noticed that the aircraft was moving along the ground, just like a motor car, only going much slower. I had no idea that aircraft could drive along on the ground. I was very surprised and excited at this. It taxied along the runway for what looked like several miles. Then it stopped, developed a more aggressive sound as the engines raced more fiercely. Before I could comprehend what was happening, the aircraft lifted off the ground. I felt as though my heart leapt right out of my mouth! There was one almighty scream, as people, who were flying for the first time, including myself, were overcome by fright!

As the back of the aircraft seemed to dip, and the front appeared to lift, I closed my eyes. I kept them tightly closed until I felt the aircraft level out once more. I opened my eyes, and looked out of the window, and was truly amazed to see how small the buildings on the ground were! They were as small as dolls houses.

It was not long before the "fasten your seat-belt" sign went off. After fumbling for a while I managed to release my seat-belt. I was somewhat surprised to find that I began to feel quite relaxed. I began to survey my "iron bird" from the inside, and was quite fascinated by it all. Soon, cool drinks were offered, which was gratefully received. It was then time to be served with a main meal. It was really an eye-opener to see this operation in progress. Trolleys being pushed along the aisles, trays of pre-cooked foods packed neatly, being handed out by very efficient staff, at record speed. It reminded me of a very busy restaurant. As I continued to observe, I noticed that the people on my right were busy pulling down their tables, I did likewise and, before I could count to three, my tray landed on my table. Somewhat baffled, I began to investigate the packages on the tray. It was amazing to find salt, pepper, cup, sugar, toothpick, wipes, knives, forks and spoon (neatly wrapped together), not to mention the main course and sweet, all neatly packed on this very small tray! I got carried away in my thoughts; I almost forgot to start eating. To my amazement, when I did start eating, the food was rather nice! *Well*, I thought to myself, *if only Tony was with me to share this unique experience, I would be so very happy.*

Meal completed, I must have fallen asleep. The next thing I knew, there was an announcement being made by the captain to say, "There was nothing to be frightened of," he was only dumping some fuel in the sea. Apparently there was some trouble with one of the engines. I was very, very, frightened. "O my God," I said, "I am going to die! I will never see my Tony again." Of course, having not flown before, made the situation worse. All manner of thoughts began to come into my head. *Dumping fuel, Why? Is it to make the aircraft lighter to help the problems? Will they start to throw some of the luggage off into the sea? What if they throw my luggage off?* I was beside myself with fright. Then I remembered what my mother had taught me. She told me that whenever I find myself in a frightening situation, I should repeat the twenty third psalm. As this came to my mind, I managed to close my eyes, calm my nerves, and silently repeated the psalm. As I was repeating the psalm, I could hear people shouting, "Lard Gad we a go dead! [Lord God, we are going to die]." Apparently, the aircraft was very close to Canada.

He landed in Newfoundland, where we spent the night at a beautiful hotel. Although I was very comfortable, I was very worried, thinking whether my friend would know that I would be landing a day late. All kinds of thoughts came into my mind. Would she contact the airport before setting out to meet me, to find out if there were any delays? What if she didn't, and turned up at the airport at the time I told her that I would be landing, and waited for hours, then return home, which was exactly what had happened.

On my arrival in England, my worst fears became a reality. No one had come to meet me. I came through customs and waited, and waited. I searched through the sea of unfamiliar faces, but there was no sight of my friend. "O my God, help me," I cried, "what am I going to do?" "Repeat the twenty third psalm," a voice said to me. I calmed myself down, sat down, closed my eyes and repeated the psalm quietly. As soon as I opened my eyes, a gentleman, who had come to meet a lady, said to me "Are you OK?"

"No," I replied. "No one has come to meet me."

"Don't worry," he said, "I am going to Victoria, I will drop you off there, and you can get a bus from Victoria to where you are going!"

"Thank-you very much," I replied. He helped me to put my very large suitcase and hand-luggage into the car, and we set-off.

On arriving at Victoria, he pulled up beside the bus-stop, took out my luggage, and told me what number bus to catch. I was shaking with nerves, everywhere looked the same to me. All the buildings looked exactly the same. *How am I going to find my friend's house? Please, God help me,* I whispered quietly.

As people went by, they turned and looked at me, all dressed up, complete with hat and gloves. Then they stared down at my large suitcase, smiled and continued along their journey. Then one very kind white lady, stopped, and said to me, "Hello, where are you going, my dear?" I showed her the address in my little note-book. "Well, it's not too far," she replied, "but how are you going to manage with that large suitcase on the bus?"

"I don't know," I said.

"I'll tell you what I will do, I will come with you." Those words were like music to my ears!

"Thank you, that is very kind of you," I said to her. After waiting a short time, the bus came along. Well, the conductor looked at me, and then looked at the suitcase. He opened his eyes so wide, as if to say, "My God what am I seeing here!" With the help of my newfound friend, I managed to get the suitcase unto the bus. My friend sat beside me, and we started chatting. Of course, her accent was so different, and she seemed to speak quite fast. I was having great difficulty understanding some of what she was saying. Soon the conductor came up to us, "Fares please."

"How much is the fare to Lewisham?" I asked. Before I could finish the sentence, a typical voice of a West Indian man came from the seat behind me, "How much is her fare?" The conductor answered. Before I could speak he opened his purse and paid my fare. My friend sitting beside me said, "I was going to pay her fare, but thank you very much." She then paid her fare. We continued chatting. Her questions were mainly about Jamaica. She wanted to know what Jamaica was like, and what made me leave the sun to come to this cold country. I must say, although I felt rather strange, dressed up like a Christmas turkey, travelling on a bus, I really did enjoy the ride. I kept looking, and observing, as we drove along. I kept thinking, *How on God's earth do people find their homes? They all look the same. Will I be able to find my home when I go shopping etc.?* At this present time, it looked an impossible task!

After sitting on the bus, for what seemed like a very long time, my friend rang the bell, and the bus stopped. We struggled to lift the very heavy suitcase off, accompanied by my pieces of hand luggage. When we got off the bus, the staring saga continued. Some people looked visibly shocked as they stared at my very large suitcase, as if to say, "What on earth has she got in that?" I was wondering how we were going to carry the suitcase to my address as I had no idea how near, or how far we had to walk from the bus stop. It was as though my friend knew that I was worried about the journey. Before I could ask her how far we had to go she

said, "Don't worry, I will manage the suitcase, as long as you
don't mind if I drag it along."

"Certainly not," I replied. As she dragged the suitcase
along the pavement I could hear a scratching and grinding.
At first, I was a bit concerned, but then I thought what the
hell, does it matter, just as long as I get this thing home!
By God's good grace, the journey was much shorter than
I anticipated. After approximately ten minutes' walk, she
stopped. "We are here," she turned and exclaimed.

"Thank God," I replied. She opened the gate and rang
the door bell.

After several rings a light-skinned West Indian lady
opened the door. She looked somewhat puzzled, "Can I help
you?" she asked.

"I hope you can," I replied. "My name is Gloria and
Lurline is expecting me. I should have arrived yesterday, but
my flight was delayed, and I had to spend the night in a
hotel in Newfoundland," I explained.

"Well Miss Lurline is not here now she's gone to work"
she replied. "Anyway, you can come in," she continued.
With a welcoming smile, she let me into the hallway. I was
so relieved to have found the address; I almost forgot to
retrieve my suitcase from my friend! The lady, my friend
and I managed to pull the suitcase up the step and into the
hallway. My friend, who I will refer to as 'an angel', gave me
a huge hug, kissed me on the cheeks and said, "Bye, I hope
you will be very happy here." Then she turned around and
walked away. With the excitement of finding my friend's
address, tinged with a sense of sadness, and loneliness, I
forgot the most important thing at that point in my life. I
forgot to ask her what her name was, and to take her address

or her telephone number! When I came to my senses, I held
my head in the palms of my hands, sighed, and muttered
to myself, "Oh no, how could I forget something so very
important!" Until this day, I cannot erase the kindness
shown to me in my hour of need in a strange country by that
lady, who I can only compare to 'an angel'. If she is still alive,
I wish above all things that she will read this autobiography
when it is published, and try to get in touch. I would dearly
love to repay her in some way for what she did for me. She
brought to me the reality of the story of the Good Samaritan
as stated in the Holy Bible. If she is no longer in the land
of the living, may God bless her spirit. I am sure that she
is continuing her good work in the spiritual world as a real
'angel' to people in distress!

After my 'angel' left, the lady said to me, "You can come
and wait in my room until Miss Lurline comes home from
work." I went in and sat down; she made me feel at ease
by striking up a conversation. She wanted to know how
Jamaica was when I left, and what job I was going to do
here in England. I tried my best to carry on the dialogue,
but the truth of the matter was that underneath that front,
I was really quite nervous. The tension increased with the
passing of the minutes! I felt quite uncomfortable in my
suit, shoes and stockings. As if she sensed my uneasiness,
she got up from her chair and said, "Would you like a cup
of tea?" "Tea?" I replied.

"Yes love; in England we drink tea all the time. You will
have to start to get used to it," she continued.

This business of drinking tea in the afternoon seemed
quite strange to me. At home, in Jamaica, we only drank
tea once a day, and that is first thing in the morning, with

breakfast. After listening to her lecture on tea drinking, I felt that I had no choice but to accept her offer of a cup of tea. I managed to smile, and then replied, "Well if tea drinking is the order of the day, I suppose that when in Rome, one has to do as the Romans' do." With that statement she went off to the kitchen. She returned to sit and continued the conversation. Before long I heard a very funny noise. "What is that?" I asked. "A the kettle a whistle". [Is the kettle whistling?]" I said, "I have never heard a kettle whistle before, because back home we don't use kettles. The water for tea is boiled in a saucepan. Can I come and see the kettle?" "Of course," she said. Off I went to the kitchen to see this mysterious whistling kettle.

Not only did I see the kettle, but I got a real eyeful; Much more than I bargained for! There were so many pots and pans, in sections, and several vegetable baskets, the small kitchen looked as though it was being used by several families. "My God, what have I let myself in for?" I said to myself in my mind. This place looked as if it is really overcrowded. My thoughts continued to race. "I wonder how many people use this one kitchen." I questioned myself. I dared not ask the lady as I was not sure how she would react to my question. She got up once more and went to the kitchen. This time she returned with a tray. On the tray she had a side-plate with some biscuits, and something which looked like a knitted woolly hat, also on the tray. I was very curious as to what that thing was; but again I was afraid to ask. *Well*, I thought, *let me wait and see what she will uncover from under that woolly hat*. With the thought still in my mind, she whisked off the woolly hat to reveal a teapot. *My God* I thought, *what next?* She poured the tea into a very large mug, put some of the biscuits on another side-plate, turned to me and said, "Come, love." The tea tasted really sweet. It was sweetened with condensed milk which I don't like because of the sweetness, but I thought I better not complain. The biscuits were also very sweet. Sweet tea and sweet biscuits, I was not amused, but I suppose beggars can't be choosers as the saying goes. Back home, that time of the day is lunch time. I am used to having a properly cooked lunch of rice, meat and vegetables, or meat patties with a milkshake, fruits of various kinds, but never tea and biscuits!

After "lunch" we continued chatting and listening to the TV. I was counting the minutes to the time when my friend would come home from work. The minutes seemed like hours! Before long, I could hardly believe my ears when the lady asked, "Would you like another cup of tea?"

"No thank-you," I said, "but I will have a cold drink if it is not too much trouble."

"No trouble at all, you can have what you like." She opened the fridge, which looked like a small white box stuck in the corner of her bedroom. My eyes popped: *welcome to madness,* I told myself. She handed me the can of drink, and went off to the kitchen to make herself another cup of tea! I sat eagerly waiting to hear the whistling of the kettle, and before many minutes had passed, it obliged me with its unique sound. From the time I entered the room until near time for my friend to come home from work, the lady must have drank approximately three or four mugs of tea!

At last evening came, and I heard the opening of the front door, followed by the slamming of the door. Then a lady's voice shouted with great excitement, "Gloria." I opened the door of the small bedroom in which I had been imprisoned for what seemed like hours. "Yes," I replied. I dashed out onto the first-floor hallway, and was greeted with the sight of my friend, leaping up the stairs; with strides that reminded me of my school days when I played hop scotch! Her efforts were rewarded with a similar reaction from me. There was an almighty clash of bodies, as we rushed into each other's arms. As we embraced and squeezed, I could hear both hearts beating as loud as a bongo drum. I was so very happy to see her, the tears just rolled down my cheeks. After some time had elapsed, we released each other from the bear hug, and managed to speak.

"What happened to you yesterday?" she asked. "I came to the airport and waited all day. I thought you had developed cold feet and decided to chicken out of coming."

"No," I replied. Then as we walked towards her room, I began to tell her my unfortunate story of my brush with death, and how I had to spend the night in a hotel. She was clearly very sorry, and apologised for not thinking of telephoning the airport before she had set out to meet me. I then told her about my encounter with my 'angel' who was sent by God to my rescue. As soon as I explained about what that white lady had done for me, she said, "Did you take her name and telephone number?"

"Unfortunately, not." I replied.

"Oh no," she said. "Some of these white people are very good," she continued. "Some of them don't like black people, especially the Jamaicans, but the majority of them are OK." The last part of her statement gave me some comfort, as I was very apprehensive about what to expect in relation to the treatment I would receive because while I was back home in Jamaica, I had heard some disturbing reports from people who had relatives or friends who had emigrated to England.

As she turned the key to open the door of her room my anticipation began to run wild! As I walked in behind her, my first thought was, *How on earth is this small room going to hold all my things that I have got in my suitcase?* It was already very overcrowded! There was a three-quarter bed, a table, a chair in one corner, dressing table and a wardrobe. There was hardly space to walk around without squeezing by some piece of furniture. Instantly I began to feel uncomfortable. *I am not accustomed to living in one room*, I thought. *Now, not only will I have to live in one room, but I will have to share a room with someone. My God, help me. How will I cope?* The expression on my face must have given my thoughts away. My friend smiled, "Don't worry," she said, "you will be alright."

"We will have a cup of tea before we do anything else," she said. I laughed out loud. "Tea!" I said. "Don't you people drink anything else except tea? I have already had a cup of tea from the lady in the next room." She laughed, "You wait till you settle down, you will soon start drinking tea like us lot," she said to me with a very lengthy laugh. Still laughing she headed towards the kitchen. Yes, you guessed right, before long there was now the familiar sound of another whistling kettle! This time I agreed to have a cup of the now famous tea. She also brought something into her room which I called a woolly hat. "What is that?" I asked.

"It's a tea cosy," she replied.

"A what?" I said.

"A tea cosy," she repeated, "it keeps the tea hot," she explained. Well I could not stop laughing. I thought it was so very funny. Then I said jokingly, "The country is so cold that even the teapots have to wear wool to keep warm." This time both of us could not stop ourselves laughing. "It's a good thing the landlady is not home," she managed to say between laughter, or she would be banging on my door telling us to stop the noise. Still laughing, she opened a packet of biscuits; I glanced at the name written on the packet, "Rich Tea," it read "Rich Tea with tea!" What a combination. Of course, I had another fit of laughter. Only this time I was laughing alone as she could not see the funny side of the joke!

Tea session completed, I was wondering how we were going to manage to carry the suitcase up the stairs. I noticed that my friend was not at all concerned. I did not know that she had a very pleasant surprise waiting for me! "Well," she said, "let me show you to your room."

"My room?" I replied. "Yes," she said. "Just before you came, someone moved out from the front room downstairs, and I got the room for you."

I was so very happy, I didn't know if I should laugh or cry. "Thank God," I said, throwing up both hands in the air. Down we went to the ground floor. She unlocked the door, and I walked in behind her into what was "my room." It was fairly clean, with a three-quarter bed, wardrobe, dressing table, a small folding dining-table, and one chair. She turned to me, "You like it?" she asked. "It's OK," I replied. I was really not over the moon with happiness at the thought that a dining-table was in the room. It was obvious that I was expected to have my meals in my room, and this was not what I was accustomed to!

After I had checked out the furniture, we sat down for a while, as she tried to strike up a conversation, which was designed to put my mind at ease. We talked for a while, and then it was time to drag the suitcase the short distance from the hallway into my room. It was a great relief that I didn't have to carry it up the stairs; for that I was extremely thankful. Suitcase firmly on the linoleum-covered floor, my friend left the room to allow me to unpack and change into something more comfortable. As I opened the suitcase and removed the first layer of clothing, a very strong smell of Captain Morgan white over-proof rum hit my nostrils! Yes you have guessed right, a small flask of the stuff, which I had wrapped in a skirt got broken, and my clothes were now drunk with the stuff! *Oh no*, I thought I had wrapped it well. I did not expect it to get broken. That small flask of rum was lovingly given to me by Tony who assured me that I would need it in the winter months to warm me up. At the sight of my precious gift now in splinters, I was so despondent; I had to fight hard to keep back the tears.

After I had finished unpacking, I went up to my friend's room. She glanced at the clock, "Well, I must start cooking the dinner," she remarked. I thought to myself that it was a bit early, as normally back home we don't have dinner until late evening. With a sense of urgency she rushed off to the kitchen, and started to prepare the stuff for cooking. As she opened the cupboards and took out the ingredients, I was pleasantly surprised to see that she had all the ingredients that we had back home! Red beans and rice, yams, green bananas, sweet potatoes, etc. I was really excited! "I didn't know that you could get these foods in England," I said to her.

"Yes man, we get everything here, except sunshine!" she replied. She let out a loud laugh. "I will correct that statement.

We do get sunshine in the summer, but the watered down version. Not hot like the sun that we get back home." She opened the fridge, which looked more like Aladdin's Cave, and out came a container in which she had well-seasoned pieces of steak. The sight of chopped thyme, curry powder, garlic and onions, to name but a few of the herbs and spices which were used to season the steak, gave me an instant feeling of from home to home! As soon as she placed the steak in the Dutch pot, she gave me another surprise. This came in the form of what we called side salad. Out came the 'beef' tomatoes (very large tomatoes), cucumber and lettuce. It was as though I was preparing dinner in my own kitchen back home. Salad prepared, she got busy mixing the carrot juice. I could not help but wonder if this was the norm, or did she have to 'go out of her way' to lay on this special Jamaican-style dinner.

The cooker had four gas rings, a grill and oven. With just us occupying the kitchen at that particular time, dinner was prepared in no time. "Go and bring up your chair," she said to me. "I only have one chair in my room!" Off I went and brought my chair up into her room. She opened up the two flaps of her small table, which had been folded in at both ends to make more space in the small over-crowded room. She managed to arrange the dishes containing the steak, rice and peas, yam, green bananas, sweet potatoes, side salad and carrot juice. We sat down and ate the lot! During the meal, I concentrated on my plate. *Where will I get all these goodies to buy,* I thought. Eventually, my thoughts got the better of me, and I had to get the answer to the information that welled up inside of me. "Where do you get these kinds of food stuffs to buy?" I asked. "No problem," she replied. "There is a place called Deptford, and another place called Brixton, you can get everything you want there; especially Brixton. What you can't get in Deptford, you are bound to get in Brixton, and if you can't get it in Brixton, you can't get it nowhere in England! Brixton market is just like a Spanish town market. The first time I went there, I had to pinch myself to make sure that I was still in England," she went on to say. "Anyway, you will see Deptford tomorrow. I have to take you down there to register you at the exchange." All this seemed like double-dutch to me, I had no idea what she was talking about. During the dialogue, I could not help but notice that she was hurrying somewhat. She suddenly cut the conversation in mid-air and started clearing the table. "I want to wash the dishes before the others come in; everybody's late tonight, they must be working overtime," she went on. I prefer to be out of here before they come in. Hurriedly, she washed and I dried up the dishes. Miraculously we finished packing away the dishes and cleaned off the cooker with just a few minutes to spare, before the rest of the household arrived home! Before long it was clear to see the reason why she was rushing to be out of the kitchen before the others came home! The others consisted of another four adults. Before long, the rush for the kitchen was in full swing. It was clearly a case of may the best man win! I was now suffering from psychological exhaustion trying to work out how on God's earth so many people managed to cook in one small kitchen, one cooker, which had only four gas rings, one oven and one grill. It seemed like a nightmare to contemplate. The irony is, that I am now involved in this case of the confusion kitchen! "Cheer up," I told myself. At least I will only have to use the kitchen on my days off, as I intended to live-in at the hospital to which I have come over to do my nurse training. With this realisation firmly in my mind, I managed to put the thought of mass over-crowding and confusion to the back of my mind.

That evening, I was very disappointed when my best friend tried to talk me out of going in for nurse training. "Listen to me," she said "Nursing don't pay money in England, and if you want to return home in five years' time, you can't do nursing, it's the least paid job in this country, and you have to work long hours, and do night work." Of course she had touched a raw nerve when she said if I want to return home in five years, that was the deadline set by myself and Tony for us to stay in England. After five years, we would return home, by that time we thought we would have saved enough money to be able to buy our own spacious house in Jamaica and live very comfortably. I was now feeling very concerned about what she had said. Apart from wanting to be a nurse from my school days, my desire was also to own my own home in Jamaica. She kept on telling me that I wouldn't be able to achieve that if I went into nursing. I was now clearly in a dilemma, because she was much older than me, and the respect that I was brought up to have for my elders, I did not want to ignore her advice. The irony was, that as soon as she introduced me to the rest of the residents, including the landlord and his wife, their first question was, "So a nursing you come up here fi do? No bother wid that missus, no money no ina nursing! [Have you come to do nursing? Don't bother to do that, there is not enough money in that profession]." I was now very concerned about my intentions. "What do I do now?" I asked myself. These people had lived in this country for some time, therefore, they must know what they are talking about. My friend was very happy when they all reiterated what she had told me. She began where they had left off, "Tomorrow morning I will take you to the exchange, and you can pick and choose jobs. There is a very nice nursing home not too far from where we live. They are always taking on people, you could get a job there if you want to do something in nursing, and they pay good money," she went on to say. By this time, I was almost agreeing with her. Then I thought of what family and friends back home would think if they knew that I was not going to nursing-school, which was what I came to do. I was in a state of confusion.

That night, I went to bed still in a state of confusion. Apart from the fact that I was now missing Tony very much, I faced another dilemma, sleeping on my own in a strange environment, in a strange country, and in a very over-crowded household. Although the house was teaming with people, I felt desperately lonely. As I reluctantly got ready for bed, I suddenly realised what I had done. The thought of sleeping on my own was almost too much to contemplate. I plucked up courage and switched off the light. Instantly I realised that the darkness in England was denser than the darkness back home! The room was pitch black. Not a glimmer of light. I then realized the reason why. You see, back home, we don't have very thick curtains, like the ones I now have at my window. We have lace curtains or window-blinds. Not a glimmer of light could penetrate these brick-wall curtains. The darkness was so dense; one could almost cut it with a knife. I was beside myself with fear of the dark. I dared not sleep with the light on. I was warned by my friend before I retired to bed not to sleep with the light on. If I did, she said, and the landlady found out, she would create merry hell. I pulled the bed-clothes over my head, and tried very hard to contain my fear of the dark, but without success. I tossed and turned for what seemed like hours. Finally, I abandoned the idea of trying to get to sleep! I got up out of bed, switched on the light, took Tony's photograph from off the mantelpiece and pressed it so very hard against my chest; it was a complete miracle the glass that encased the photograph was not shattered. The atmosphere quivered with hysteria, as I held the photograph against my chest. I was unable to control my emotions, and the tears just ran down my cheeks. Remembering Tony's words, which now sounded like church bells in my ears. "If going to England will make you happy, I won't stand in your way." At this moment in time, I wished that he had stood in my way! If he had, I would not now be in this state of utter hysteria. Yes, I did leave the light on until almost daybreak. There was no way I could sleep in that dense darkness alone! *Decisions, decisions*, I thought. I must make a decision this morning, whether to go into nursing-school, or to take the advice of my friend and the entire household and go and work in the nursing home that they all insist I go to work in.

For the next few days my thoughts worked overtime to come to a concrete decision. Finally, I decided to go along to the nursing home to see for myself what I was letting myself in for. I arrived there one morning, and asked to speak to the matron. "We don't have matrons here, me dear," answered the young pretty nurse. "We have a charge nurse," she continued. "You looking for a job?" she asked. "Yes," I replied. "I was told that there are vacancies here," I continued. "Well I think so," she replied, "but let me go and have a word with the charge nurse," she asked me to wait for a moment. As I stood against the window in the very long corridor, I started to survey the grounds of the nursing home. It was very beautiful. There were beautiful lawns, lots of flower gardens and lots of healthy looking trees. Well, I said to myself, the grounds are indeed very attractive. I wonder what the inside is like.

After what seemed like hours, the nurse came back. The charge nurse will see you in her office." She walked me along the corridor, and then she stopped at a door on the left, and knocked. "Come in," replied a woman's voice with a very strange accent. I entered the office, and sitting round a large desk was a very large lady dressed in a nurse's uniform. She smiled at me, "Sit down," she said. I sat down and smiled back at her. "I hear you are looking for a job?" "Yes," I replied. "Well I have some vacancies, but it is shift work, and sometimes you have to work nights." At the mention of nights, I opened my eyes wide! She must have noticed the surprised look on my face. She smiled and re-assured me, "It's not too bad on nights, and you will like it." "You can start Monday if you want the job!" "I will take it," I replied. She then discussed salary, working schedules, and so on. Then, when the formalities were finished, she took me to the uniform room, which was called sewing room in those days, to have me fitted out with my uniforms. I must confess that I felt quite proud as I admired myself in the mirror in my nurse's uniform. I looked just like a real nurse! You have to make sure that your caps are well starched and properly ironed, and if you feel that you can't do them well, there is a laundry service which does your dresses and caps, but most of the nurses like to do their caps themselves. You must wear

lace-up black shoes and black stockings/tights at all times.
"Tights?" I asked, "What is that?" She then explained what
tights were.

Uniform fitting completed, she proceeded to show me
around the nursing home. Initially I was quite shocked at
what I saw. I had no idea that there were so many old people
who were in need of love and care, and altogether in one
home! I was almost moved to tears as I was introduced to
some of the more mentally alert patients. Some of them gave
me a smile, some squeezed my hands, and the less alert ones
just stared or were quite oblivious of my presence. Those dear
old folks brought back with a mighty thump the memory of
my beloved grandad. I felt as though I couldn't wait until
Monday morning to start caring for them! I wanted to put
on my uniform and get started there and then. The most
homely area of that home was the kitchen. It was just like a
large family kitchen, only with much more utensils. There
were boxes of all types of breakfast cereals, lots of loaves
of bread, butter, dozens of eggs, jams, and marmalade,
everything that one would find in the kitchen of an ordinary
household. There were also dozens of cups and saucers, and
some plastic cups with a spout. I enquired of one of the
nurses what they were. She explained to me that they were
used to feed the patients who needed to be fed by the nurses.
They were also used by patients who could feed themselves
but who had difficulty drinking from an ordinary cup. It
prevented them from spilling the drink onto themselves.
Tour completed, I said goodbye and left.

As I walked home – fortunately for me, the nursing
home was within walking distance from where I lived –
all kinds of thoughts raced through my mind. Thought

number one was, where in the world did the charge nurse"
originate from? The accent is so strange, it's almost like
singing. I knew one thing for sure, she was not from Jamaica.
Thought number two, how comes so many old folks were
in-residence in that nursing home? Why are they not looked
after by their children or the rest of the family? How could
so many old folks not have any family or any children to
look after them in their old age? You see, where I come
from, the care of the elderly is entirely the responsibility of
the family. This was a great shock to my system! I could
hardly wait for my friend to come home from work to find
out the answer to the reason why. By this time I was very
emotionally distressed. As I walked along, I could see in my
mind's eye the smiles, the sadness, the obliviousness on the
faces of those dear old souls. It made me both sad and happy
at the same time. It was sad to think that they are away
from the love of their own family and friends to be looked
after by strangers, and happy because I will be one of those
strangers who will have the privilege of sharing in their care.
It was with a great struggle that I finally arrived home. I
had made several wrong turnings and had to stop and ask
someone the right direction as all the houses looked the
same to me, so did the streets. My first long-distance walk
on the streets of London was a real nightmare! In my quest
to find my address, I went to enquire from a man working
in a butcher's shop. He came outside, pointed across the
next street, and replied, "You can see it from here luv." He
smiled and turned back into the shop. Needless to say, I felt
quite silly! The silliness intensified when I later realised that,
that was to be my local butchers. The trouble was, the first
time that I went there to do some shopping, he remembered

me. As soon as I entered the door, he laughed. At the end of my shopping, he joked, "You think you can find you way home?"

I have jumped the gun a bit, but never mind. I now return to my arrival home from my visit to the nursing home. Still in a state of complete shock, I managed to make myself a cup of English tea, which I had with some Rich Tea biscuits. I am now already getting into the tea drinking habit. It gradually grows on you. As I sipped my freshly made brew, and munched into the crisp biscuits, I could not stop my thoughts from returning to the residents in that nursing home. *Please God*, I thought, *don't allow me to stay here in England, until I become old. Help me, Jesus, to return to Jamaica within five years maximum!* After my tea and biscuits, I tried to gather myself together as best I could, and started to prepare my dinner so that I could get out of the kitchen before the multitude came home from work, and the stampede for the kitchen started. I finished in the nick of time!

Boy was I glad to see my friend home from work. I had so many burning questions overcrowding my mind, to which I hoped she was able to give me the answers to! As soon as she opened the door, I rushed to greet her. Just like a small child eagerly awaiting the arrival of their mother home from work. "Hi," she remarked, "how did the interview go?"

"Very well," I replied, "I got the job and I can start on Monday if I want it," I replied.

"Good" she replied. "Take it, work and throw partner (a system where one saves a certain amount of money every week along with a number of other people. One person is responsible to collect the monies each week and then gives the monies collected to the respective individuals each week.

A record of the transactions is kept. The person responsible is called the 'banker.' "That way," she continued, "you will save up enough money quick, and you can go back home in no time. You can write to Tony now and tell him to get ready to join you," she went on. "At least you don't have to worry about accommodation; you have a nice big front room." If only she could read my thoughts, she would hear me saying, *And one more person to add to the already over-crowded environment!*

I found myself in another dilemma! Although what I wanted more than anything in the world was for my husband to join me, I dare not send and tell him what the living conditions were like. If I did, he would refuse to come and, certainly his advice to me would be, "Come home." I did not show any emotion, I just calmly replied, "Well I will have to think it over," and left it at that.

I re-opened the conversation with, "Tell me something if you can, how come so many old people end up in that nursing home?"

"Well, my dear, this country is a different kettle of fish, it's not like Jamaica. Here if old people don't have anybody to look after them, the government take over. There is social security, welfare, housing benefit, NHS, and all sorts." I had no idea what she was talking about! She could see the bewilderment in my eyes. At that point she started to explain the services one by one. I was completely amazed! "How very fortunate the people living in this country are," I exclaimed. I could hardly believe my ears when she explained that if people are not working, the government gave them money to buy food, and help them with paying their rent, some even get rent free accommodation!

I then went on to describe the way the charge nurse that interviewed me spoke; almost like singing. I did my very best to put on an example of the way she spoke. My friend laughed so much; she almost fell off her chair! "That sounds like smallie she chuckled.

"What do you mean 'smallie'," I replied.

"One of the small islands," she answered. "They don't like Jamaicans, and Jamaicans don't like them. Them think Jamaicans is too cheeky (rude), and Jamaicans think that they are too soft. At their place of work they don't stand up for themselves, they are yes-men and yes-women! Make sure you don't call them 'Small Island'. There have been lots of fights between them and Jamaicans. Some of them lost their jobs because of the name calling." I found that quite stupid. As far as I am concerned, it doesn't matter which of the islands you come from, we are all West Indians firstly, and secondly we are all immigrants in a foreign country, and we are all God's children. I really didn't think it was funny. I certainly was not laughing as I couldn't see the joke.

Before the week was completed, I had another eye-opener (surprise). I was awakened by banging of what sounded like tins, and the boisterous revving of what sounded like the engine of a truck! I got out of bed, peered through the window and to my horror I saw white men emptying dustbins! "My God," I gasped, "What are white men doing emptying dustbins!" They had on blue overalls, and were wearing dirty scruffy shoes, and dirty gloves. I was completely gob-smacked (lost for words). I could not believe my eyes! I had this pre-conceived idea of what kind of jobs white people were supposed to do, and emptying rubbish bins was certainly not one of them! Back home the few white men that I knew were property owners, business men, or heads of establishments, such as banks, building societies, headmasters, or priests. They lived in huge houses on acres of well fruited land, and employed maids. Depending on the size of the family, some had a cook, a separate maid that did the washing and ironing, a nursemaid for the children, and a yard-boy that looked after the garden and to do odd chores. If they are cattle farmers, or fruit producers, or own sugar cane plantations, they would most certainly employ several workers, including rangers, which rode around on horses carrying shot-guns!

I was pleasantly surprised to see milkmen driving around in open carts, which were called 'milk-floats.' They would park the milk-floats/milk-carts, jump out and leave the vehicle unattended, sometimes they would be quite a few houses up the road from where they left their milk-float delivering their 'pints', as the glass pint bottles of milk were referred to. These milk-floats would even be parked around the corner where the milkmen could not observe them, and they would be happily delivering their "pints!" I was overwhelmed by the trust placed in the community, that they would not help themselves to the odd "pint!" I thought to myself, if they did that in JA (short for Jamaica), they would return to find a "pintless" milk-float! It wasn't long before I was having my "pints" delivered to my front door. I almost forgot to say that the milkman was white. People, who were working, would return from work in the evening, to find their "pints" still sitting on their door-step. The milk bottles were washed out and left on the door-step for collection by the friendly milkman. There was always a clatter as the milkman would collect as many empty milk bottles in one go as he could carry. There was a milk bottle on the end of each finger! Milk was not the only thing the milkman delivered, one could get fruit juice, bread, eggs and potatoes from the friendly milkman. If the milkman called after residents had left for work, these items would be left on the door-step, along with the pints of milk, and all would be still intact when the rightful owners arrived at whatever time! If one was going away on holiday, they would write a note, fold it neatly, and stick it into the empty milk bottle for the milkman. "No milk please until…" Or if one needed extra pints or fewer pints the same note writing procedure would apply. The milkman is usually late on a Friday and on Saturday morning. Those were the two mornings when he carried out his collection of monies owed for milk delivered throughout the week. On those two mornings, there would be intensive activity, as the iron gates banged, and the wooden gates made a squeak as they "flew" back into their hinges as the milkman darted in and out through gates, ringing doorbells. Women would often appear at front doors clad in night-gowns and bed slippers, and hair in rollers. Soon the pockets of the blue and white striped apron of the milkman would be bulging with half-pennies, pennies, three pennies, six pennies, shillings and two shilling pieces.

The rest of the week was spent trying to find my way around. I always use a landmark to remind me where to get off the bus, such as a shop, a special building, a school, and so on. Even then, I would often go past my stop! Looking back now, it was quite funny. During my few free days before I started working, I did a lot of shopping. Food was very cheap. One could do so much shopping with a few pounds! A loaf of bread was about sixpence, meat was extremely cheap and one would get soup meat, which was the bony parts of beef, thrown in for free when one bought steak. Gradually, I would buy my cooking utensils, and then I would graduate to buying things such as clothes iron, ironing-board and bed clothes. Bed clothes were easy to accumulate. In those days, Indians who were called "salesmen" would go around with large suitcases on their heads knocking on doors, selling bedclothes. One only needed to give them a few shillings deposit, and your bedclothes problem would be taken care of. They would then give you a little book with your total amount owed. They would then call every week to collect a small amount. I often heard of folks who would hide from the salesmen. If they didn't have the money to pay when the salesman ring the doorbell, they would keep quiet and would not open their doors; thus pretending not to be at home! After a while these salesmen would graduate from walking with suitcases on their heads, to driving a car or sometimes a van. I have still got in my possession beautiful bedspreads with matching pillowcases bought from those salesmen of the 60s. These are treated with great respect as they are now antique and very special. I still am the proud owner of a large Bible bought from those salesmen, which is as new. The reason for its excellent condition is that it is too heavy for everyday use. I just keep it open on a small table in my bedroom. Once in a while I kneel down and read from this most treasured book in the kneeling position, as it is much too large and heavy to hold and read in the usual way. It has now become a unique spiritual reminder of the 1960s.

I will never, ever, forget my very first day at work in that nursing home. After I was shown around, I was asked to wash and dress this old white gentleman, and get him out of bed for his breakfast. I went to the bathroom, collected a washbowl, and half filled it with nice warm water, as I was instructed by the nurse who was in charge of the ward (a white nurse). I then went up to the old man's bed, pulled the curtains around him and said, "Good morning Mr. Jones, how are you?"

"F… Off," he shouted. "Go back to the jungle where you came from, and leave me alone." His outburst was followed by an almighty kick which landed in my tummy. I was doubled up in pain and was unable to move for some time. He then spat at me. As if that was not bad enough, he then gave the locker an almighty kick sending the bowl of water flying! At that point I dashed out from behind the curtains and went to find the nurse who had asked me to attend to him. I found her in the kitchen preparing the patient's breakfasts. I told her what had happened; she laughed and said, "Mr. Jones is like that; he doesn't like coloured people!" She went over to his bed, gave him a talking to, and told him to apologise to me. "Sorry," he said. He was then as good as gold. I washed and dressed him, got him out of bed and fed him his breakfast. During my stay on that ward, Mr Jones and I became great friends. No more swearing, kicking or spitting!

Soon I was in the swing of things, I loved caring for those old folks; I treated them just like my grandparents. There was one problem; I had great difficulty understanding when they spoke. It took me quite some time to get into some of the slangs. I would say yes when I should have being saying no! Once the nurse said to me "You didn't understand what I said, did you?"

"You are saying no when you should be saying yes. Take your time and listen or you could get into trouble!"

My very first month's pay seemed like a lot of money, around forty pounds. Forty pounds in those days was quite a lot of money. From that I paid my rent, I did not have to punch my electricity or gas. The rent was all inclusive at that house. I will come to the electric and gas punching situation later on when I left that address! I also did my shopping, which included a gradual replacement of household items which I left back home, save five pounds (5.00) per week in a partner/savings club.

I explained earlier on how this worked. All this was accomplished with relative ease. Apart from missing Tony, I began to feel fairly settled. I could see that when he joined me and start to work as an accountant, we could save up quite fast and perhaps would be able to return home before my target of five years!

I couldn't help but notice that as I travelled around London, visiting the stores, open markets, shops and supermarkets etc., that there was a complete lack of colourful clothing. I looked like a Christmas tree, which was all lit up, in comparison to the drab colours worn by the English. I couldn't help but notice that people would stare at me when I was out and about, sometimes with a smile which said, "I admire your multi-coloured dress, I wish I could wear something like that." Or the stare which said, "Oh my God, that looks ghastly I couldn't wear that, all we need now are the palm trees!" My brightly coloured summer dresses were certainly an eye opener to the English ladies. Thank goodness I was not the only Caribbean lady who was dressed in bright colours. It was almost like introducing a completely new trend of dressing to London. Now thirty-seven years later, I have

seen the complete death of the drab blacks and browns,
these have been replaced with very bright colours! I still
look with amazement during the summer months at the
array of bright coloured summer dresses and sandals on the
streets of London. It is fascinating to see that even the men
had caught on to the "bright colour" act. Men now wear
brightly coloured shirts and ties, which was never heard of
in the 1960s! In the summer months, one could change
the name London, to Jamdon! Got it? London, Jamaica.
London/Jamdon! There is a saying, 'what a difference a day
makes'. I can say, "What a difference the years make," and
that is speaking from my own experience.

After three months had passed, which looked to me
more like three years, it was time to ask Tony to join me in
England! It was a very difficult decision in mainly two ways.
One, what if he doesn't like it here, and two, what if he can't
cope with living in one room with so many other people
sharing one kitchen, and one bathroom. Oh, and thirdly,
living in a house where the landlord is also in-resident! I
was in a real dilemma. It was as the saying goes 'between the
devil and the deep blue sea!' I decided to take a gamble, and
send and ask him to join me. He replied to say he would. As
soon as I got the letter of agreement, I was busy shopping for
winter clothing for Tony as it would be winter by the time he
joined me. I then began to count the days to Tony's arrival.
I hung the long black winter coat that I bought for Tony
outside my wardrobe, and positioned the black wool-lined
winter boots where I could see them as soon as I entered the
room, to constantly remind me that Tony's coming was now
a reality, and that I only have to be lonely for another few
weeks!

I was praying that I could find another large front room at a different address in a house with less people sharing the bathroom and kitchen before Tony arrived. It wasn't long before my prayers were answered! Someone told me that a very large front room was up for rent not far from where I was living, and that it was not too over-crowded. Just the landlord and his wife, another young couple, and two brothers lived there. I decided to go and check it out. The house was very nice from the outside, with posh net curtains at the windows, and the door-knocker was brass which was well polished, so much so, that it shone like gold. On closer examination, there was a very posh door mat at the front door. This struck me as a place that I would like to live. Apart from the seemingly well-kept appearance, the rent was much less than what I was paying at the moment. I decided to return in the evening when the landlord and his wife were home from work to find out if they would let me the room. I was comforted by the fact that I had in my position enough money to pay the one month's rent in advance, as was the custom. "Please God, let me get that room," I prayed. I could hardly wait for evening to come to find out if I was successful. Finally, it was evening. I gave them a couple of hours to prepare their evening meal, and eat. I knew that when one returned home from work, one just wanted to get that meal ready, eat, and have a cup of tea, then put one's feet up, settle down and watch the TV. I knew that if the room was still vacant, God wouldn't let anyone go around acquiring it before I did. I also knew that after a meal and a cup of tea, the landlord would be in a better frame of mind to do the transaction. I waited until the time was right, then I dressed myself, and went around to find out if I was lucky.

I rang the doorbell, not too loud; I was told some people don't like it when you ring their doorbell too loudly; so I gave what one could call a moderate ring. Not too loud, but loud enough that they could hear while watching TV. The front door was opened and I was confronted by a middle-aged coloured lady, very refined, and wearing the broadest smile. "Can I help you," she asked. "Yes please," I replied. "I have come to ask about the room that I was told that you have for rent."

"Come in," she said. As soon as she said, "Come in," I knew then that the room was still vacant. As I entered in, I noticed that the hall was covered with red lino, this also covered the stairs. The lino was so very well polished; one could almost use it as a mirror!

I followed her into the dining-room. "Sit yourself down," she said. "I will just go and fetch my husband." She returned with a very handsome man with light complexion, wearing a broad smile. "This is my husband," she went on. "Hello, how are you?" he said. "Fine, thank you," I replied. "So you've come about the room," he went on. "Yes," I said. "Well the room is still vacant at the moment. My wife will deal with it," he continued. The impression he gave me, was one of a very easy going quiet, well cultured man. He sat down, as his wife told me the price of the room, and all her rules and regulations! She gave me the impression of a very fussy, bossy, domineering lady! After she finished laying down the law, she asked, "Do you still want the room?"

"Can I see it" I said. "Of course," she replied. I followed her up the well-polished lino-covered stairs. The room was at the front of the house, immediately above her room.

It was very large, well furnished, with very expensive lace curtains and very posh lined heavy curtains. The walls were covered with red flax wallpaper, which looks like red velvet! Regardless of her attitude, I fell in love with the room. I am sure she was taking note of the smile on my face. I glanced at her, and I could see that she was also smiling! "You like it?" she asked. "Very much," I replied. She then went on to point at the rest of the rooms on that floor and told me the names of the occupants. Then it was time to show me around the bathroom and toilet. My room was very close to the bathroom. This could be to my advantage. I thought, *If I am quick on the draw, as the saying goes, I could be the first to make it to the bathroom in the mornings!* On the other hand, the rest of the household could be thinking what I am thinking, and could be up very early, before I did, thus beating me to the draw! It boils down to a matter of the best man wins. We returned to the ground floor through the dining room, to the kitchen, which was very small, with very little storage space, a small gas cooker with four rings and an oven. The first thing that came to my mind was how on God's earth am I going to manage my cooking with any kind of comfort in this very small kitchen, which is shared by so many people, including Miss Fuss Pot! The thought of it was too much to contemplate. There was hardly enough space to swing a cat, as the saying goes. For a split second my mind focused back on the cooking facility at my present address, and I began to wonder if it were a case of out of the frying-pan, into the fire! I quickly gathered my thoughts. *Well it seems that's how it is in England* I consoled myself. *When in Rome, do as the Romans do*. Again my thoughts raced off. If I had the slightest idea that this was how the living conditions were in England, I would not even have thought about coming to this country. My concept of the streets of London being paved with Gold went right out the window! She then opened the door which led from the kitchen to the back garden. A small well-kept garden with two short clothes lines for drying the washing, in the summer of course. This was another hurdle. How will these two short clothes lines be adequate for such a large house hold? What if it is a nice day and everybody decided to do some washing? There was the public laundromat, but I don't like the idea of washing my clothes in the public laundry. I have heard stories of people washing all kinds of filthy clothes in those public washing machines! My friend told me that when she takes her laundry to the public laundry, she almost uses a whole bottle of Dettol in the washing machine!

After agreeing to comply with all her in-house rules, which included cleaning and polishing the dining-room floor alternatively each week, this rule involved all the tenants, even the two brothers, this was a great climb down for me, because at home, I am used to having a maid to do the cleaning of floors etc. On the one hand I felt happy getting the room, but on the other hand I felt sad, having to come down to the level of a maid. Cleaning someone's floor! I thank God that I was never one to mistreat my maids back home. Again I had no idea that when one rents accommodation in England, one had to take on the tasks of cleaning the landlord's floors; if only I knew, I would never, never, have come to this country!

I paid her one month's rent in advance, smiled nicely, told her many thanks for letting me have the room, and left.

I then made arrangements to move in the following week. It was not a complicated move, as I only had to pack my clothing, ironing board and cooking utensils.

A few days after moving in, I began to feel uneasy. This lady would watch my every move. Not just myself, but I noticed that she acted that way towards all the tenants. She gave me the impression that she wanted the rent, but she did not like anyone sharing her kitchen or her bathroom! She would check behind you every time you used the bathroom, to make sure that you cleaned the sink and the bath, and that there was not a single drop of water on her precious bathroom lino-covered floor! I often heard her mumbling to herself, "These people won't wash out the sink after they use it," "They always drop water on the floor," etc. She would grumble loud enough for others to hear, yet she would not confront one and say so to their faces! That was what I thought. Of course, that was not the case. I soon found out that she was a right battle axe. Her mumbling was because I was a newcomer, and she did not want to show me her true colours so soon after I had moved in!

After a few weeks her mumbling reverted back to her usual shouting and cursing. Not at me, thank God, but at all the other tenants. I told you earlier on, about the young girl who lived with her boyfriend. Well, I honestly don't think that there was a day when she and this lady were not shouting, screaming and swearing at each other. It was quite frightening and unnerving. Once they got into a fight in the kitchen!

When the fighting ceased, the young lady invited me into her room to have a cup of tea with her and her boyfriend. I took the opportunity to ask her what had caused the fight. She related to me that the landlady was a very jealous woman. She doesn't like to see her husband talk to anyone. She went on to say that the husband was a very kind person, and that on a Friday evening, on his return from work, he would always bring something for all the tenants, a mango, apples, or whatever. Of course, the wife did not like it, and would wait for the opportunity to find something to start an argument with the tenants. This particular fight broke out because of the way that she cleaned and polished the dining-room floor! She went on to say, that it had been her week to polish the floor, and there was a small piece of carpet in the middle of the dining-room. Of course, the dining-room table and chairs are on the piece of carpet, so she did not bother to disturb the piece of carpet, she just polished the lino around the carpet and, of course, when Miss Fuss Pot, as I sometimes refer to her, came in from work, she went straight to the piece of carpet, lifted it up to see if the young lady had cleaned under it, and, of course, she did not, as she thought it was not necessary. Of course, she flew into the kitchen where the young lady was preparing her dinner, and ordered her to go and clean under the piece of carpet. An argument broke out, followed by the fight!

I could hardly believe my ears! *How silly can one get?* I thought. How is it possible to live in the same house with someone and not talk to the person, share a joke or a cup of tea!

I began to wonder how long it would be before she started to pick on me, and how could I avoid speaking to her husband! The trouble was her husband was a very friendly person. He loved to talk, and had a permanent smile. He also had the most infectious laugh one could encounter. It was very hard for one not to warm to his personality.

Back in the sixties, it was customary for house-owners to set aside a room, usually in the basement, where they would set up a club, mainly to accommodate Afro-Caribbean people. There one would find a "back home" atmosphere. Curried goat and rice, green boiled bananas and salted mackerel, patties, red-stripe beer, soft drinks and, of course, Jamaican white rum. One would also find comfortable chairs and tables, where one could relax, have a drink, and a chat. As usual the main topic would be about the weather, the landlord, or the workplace. One had a choice of having a chat, listening to music, or if one so desired, have a dance. It was a great way of getting rid of the stress encountered at the work-place and at the over-crowded house where one had to spend many unhappy hours.

I can remember the very first time that I visited one of those "house clubs" as they were called. It was in the basement of a house in Lewisham, South London. It was summertime. I remember exclaiming how beautiful and warm the night was. As I strolled along, with other members of the household, dressed only in a cotton dress and sandals, the night wind gently blowing through my long hair, which I had coloured auburn, for a split second I could almost convince myself that I was strolling along in my home-town back home! Since my arrival in England, I never went out at night. Therefore, it was a real shock to my system to experience walking around after ten o'clock at night dressed in light clothing. For that short moment I felt truly happy! All that was missing was "Tony" by my side. Of course, this moment of happiness was due to my landlady's husband, who invited all the tenants out to this "house club" for a night out.

On entering the club, there was a "home from home" feeling. Everybody was greeted with a friendly hello. We were really made to feel welcome. My eyes were busy taking in the scene as the saying goes at home. I was introduced to the owners, and to other club members. I could tell that my landlady and her husband were regulars. He immediately started chatting to the other members, and belted out his infectious laugh! He then walked over to where we were sitting and took the orders. Some wanted curried goat and rice, some patties; others wanted boiled green bananas and salted mackerel. I had curried goat and rice. After we finished eating, my landlady's husband went up to the juke-box and put on some lovely records. He then started to dance with his wife. Other people joined in. At that point I felt as though I was the loneliest young woman in the whole world! Yes, you guessed right, I was the only person sitting down. Everybody was now on the dance floor. I remember the record that they were dancing to as clear as day. "Knock three times on the ceiling if you want me." I could hardly bear to watch the couples on the dance floor. Oh if only Tony was here, I thought. The irony was that was one of our favourite records!

Although I wanted to dance very much, I was praying inwardly that my landlady's husband did not ask me to dance. The thought was still in my mind when the record stopped, and he sat his wife down and, yes, you guessed right, he walked over to me and asked me to dance, after he had put the same record on again! I wanted to say no but did not want to appear unsociable. As we danced, I kept looking over my shoulder at the expression on his wife's face. It was not a happy one! I could hardly wait for the record to finish so that I could sit down. For the remainder of the night one could cut the atmosphere between her and her husband with a knife! She became very snappy, and hardly spoke to me. In fact, she hardly spoke to anyone who was in the club. She completely cut herself off; except for the odd word to her still happy and talkative husband.

I must honestly say that that night out was a complete disaster for me. For the rest of the night I felt really uncomfortable. Although I was in a very happy atmosphere with good music, good back-home food, and friendly people, I suddenly felt quite alone. From the end of that dance, the only happy moment for me was when the juke-box played the closing record, Goodnight my Love; Pleasant Dreams, Sleep Tight my Love'. I could hardly wait to get home to my lonely front room, with Tony's brand new and unworn winter clothing, and his photograph on the mantelpiece, squeeze it against my chest and whisper, "Oh Tony, if only you were here with me." Suddenly I felt the tears well up into my eyes, and before I realised what was happening, the tears began to flow down my cheeks. At that point, I became engulfed in a sudden onset of homesickness. If it was possible to go to a travel service at that very moment and book an immediate flight home, I would have done so! After some time had elapsed, I managed to pull myself together, got undressed, and got into bed.

As I had said earlier, my room was immediately above my landlady's room. To add to my frustration, I could hear her and her husband having a raging argument. *My God*, I thought to myself, *I hope that argument is not over the dance that her husband had with me. If that is the reason, I am now quite sure that it won't be long before she starts to find a way to get her revenge on me!* She was that type of vindictive sophisticated lady; my hunch was right on key. The very next day, I began to notice that she was a bit cold towards me. I was not overreacting, because the other tenants noticed it as well! The young girl with which she had the fight, laughed and remarked, "G it's your turn now. Watch out! You are now in her jealous book."

"She doesn't know me," I replied, "because I am living alone, I am not looking for a man. The only man I am looking forward to having is my beloved husband. By the grace of God, it won't be long before he joins me, and she will see how dark and handsome my husband is, and hopefully she will realise that there is no comparison."

During that week my anticipation of Tony's arrival reached boiling point. It had gotten to the point where I felt as though I really couldn't cope another day without Tony's company. I was by now almost paranoid with the thought of his coming. So much so, that I sent him a cable which read, "Missing you terribly, please come quickly." That's how desperate I was. Sending a cable was the last thing that I wanted to do, because I can remember that when I was back home, cables seldom bring good news! When one gets a cable, one automatically fears the worst, so much so that some people on receiving a cable would burst into tears before they opened it. Some would even faint, while others would ask someone to open and read the contents of the cable for them, as they would be much too afraid to open and read it for themselves! I was very sorry to put my beloved husband in that situation, but that was the only way I could let him know how much I was missing him.

Within a couple of days, I received a cable from Tony which read, "Miss you too, darling; will come as soon as I can. Love, Tony. Those were the most comforting words I had heard for a very long time. I would read that cable over and over, and over again, and again, and again. It was such consolation to know that Tony was really coming soon and that I was not going to be on my own for much longer. During those lonely days waiting for Tony's coming, made me aware of the utter loneliness, and dense emptiness, some people experience by living on their own. It is not something that I would recommend to anyone. I certainly couldn't handle it on a long term basis.

You remember earlier on that I had said, when I was leaving Jamaica to come to England, I had sold some of my furniture to assist me with my fare, and various expenses. Well, most of the furniture was sold on a credit basis. The buyers would give me some of the asking price, and I would then have to chase them for the remainder. I already mentioned earlier on how difficult a situation that was. On several occasions when I called to collect monies owing, the person who owed me the money would be at home, but would keep very quiet, and would not answer, pretending not to be at home. That persisted until the very day before I left Jamaica. I left without getting all the monies owing. Shortly after receiving Tony's cable, I had a letter from him to say he was still unable to collect most of the monies outstanding on articles bought by people before I left, and that he doesn't think that they had any intention of paying up. I was not a happy person when I read that letter because those were people who I knew for many years, and who had appeared to be honest and trustworthy, but obviously that was not the case. I wrote back to tell Tony not to worry about the outstanding debt owing to us. Forget about it, but to be assured that one day, those people who think that they are being smart by avoiding payment will, one day, lose more than what they owe us. My dear mother always used this statement from the Bible, "What one sows, one will also reap." One cannot sow peas, and expect to reap corn, which was her explanation of the Bible quotation.

I was anxiously anticipating Tony coming, so much so, that it wouldn't have mattered whether they paid up or not. I didn't have to wait much longer before I received the long-awaited letter to say that Tony had booked his flight. The letter also contained flight number, terminal, date and time of landing etc. When I received that letter I could not contain myself! My joy was unspeakable. Words are inadequate to explain the joy that welled up inside me. I can honestly say that the days leading up to the date of Tony's arrival were the longest I had ever experienced. One day seemed like a whole week, and one week seemed like a month. The nights appeared twice as long, as I was unable to sleep. I would lay awake most part of the night just thinking about Tony, and how wonderful it will be to be together again. It got to a point that I had to force myself to eat. I would cook the most delicious meal, sit at the table, took one look at the meal, and promptly went straight off it. I completely lost my appetite!

Finally, the great day arrived, and it was time to go to meet my beloved Tony. I had made arrangements with a friend, who knew someone with a car, and would collect me on the day in question to go to meet Tony. Well, the night before the great day, I am sure that I did not sleep for eight minutes without waking up to check the time, although I had set the alarm to go off, I did not trust to completely rely on my alarm clock! I was so afraid that I would oversleep.

I kept reading the flight ticket to make sure that Tony was really on his way to join me in England, and that I was not just imagining it.

At last it was daybreak, needless to say, I was up long before the alarm clock went off! It wouldn't have mattered anyway whether it went off or not, I hadn't slept for most of the night anyway. I sprang out of bed, had a wash before anyone could get to the bathroom, had a cup of tea, and got ready. I could not tolerate even a few cornflakes; my stomach just could not cope. At this point, my heart was in control! My heart beat must have increased from the normal eighty beats per minute to about one hundred! My pulse began to race, and I was just so very, very, happy. I kept thinking, *Tony is coming, Tony is coming, I am not dreaming, this is for real.* Even now, as I tap out these words on my typewriter, I can remember how excited I was then, as if it was yesterday. The love I had for my husband was very unique.

Finally, there was the tooting of a car horn outside my front door, and I knew then that it was the driver who had come to collect me to take me to the airport to meet my beloved. Nervously, I descended the steps leading from the first floor to the ground floor, my knees trembling with excitement, my hands shaking. I opened the front door to be greeted by a smiling gentleman, and the now familiar greeting of, "Alright?" to which I replied, "Yes, thank-you." I had the winter coat, gloves, scarf and winter boots that I had bought for Tony. "Your husband is a very lucky man," he exclaimed, "I can see that he will be well taken care of," he continued.

Without further ado, we set off along the semi quiet streets, occupied mainly by early rising milkmen and their milk-floats. We also passed several women waiting at the bus stops. I could not understand what they were doing standing at bus stops so early in the morning, some were on their own! I enquired from the driver what their purpose was. He told me that they were early morning office cleaners. He went on to explain that most women, both black and white, and even men, would do early morning office cleaning, which meant that they would be up very early and travel to clean offices around London. Some would do this instead of working in factories, while others would do so and finish in time to start their regular jobs, thus giving them that little bit of extra cash. I thought to myself, *I have a lot to learn about this wonderful country!*

Soon we were out of the town centres and onto the M1 motorway. That was an experience I will never forget. It was quite foggy, but the drivers seemed to ignore the fog, and were just, what seemed to me, like speeding along. It was quite frightening. The main source of lighting were small lights on the road, which reminded me of what we call 'blinkes,' or 'fire flies,' back home. These are small fly-like creatures which fly about in the dark with very bright lights. In the dark one can't see anything of them except for the bright light. They are really beautiful to watch as they flicker about in the dark. I was informed that those lights on the road were called 'cat's eyes!' They seemed to adorn the motorway for miles, and were a beautiful sight to behold.

At last we arrived at the airport, and I alighted from the back seat of the car clutching Tony's winter coat etc. I was very surprised to see how busy the airport was so early in the morning. It seemed like a sea of faces dragging suitcases on wheels by their straps, pushing trolleys packed with luggage, scrambling along with hand luggage over their shoulders, accompanied by further pieces of luggage in their hands! It was an amazing sight. The driver and I had to literally fight our way through the deluge of people to the inquiry desk to get some information regarding Tony's flight arrival. Luckily we were early and had to wait quite a while as the flight was delayed. We passed the time away by sipping coffee which we bought from the airport canteen. As we sipped the freshly made coffee, which I must say tasted very nice, I told him a bit about Tony and how eager I was awaiting his arrival. He also told me quite a lot about England, as he had been living here for some time. Needless to say some things which he told me were quite shocking. Others were well received, as I was what he called, "Just come!" Some of the information summoned a laugh, other's a smile, and some I did not think at all funny.

Although we were deep in conversation, I could not help but notice the variety of nationalities which were arriving at the arrival gate. It was a real eye-opener, Afro-Caribbean, Indians, Africans, people from the Far-East, Europeans, etc. I could now see why back home they called England the mother land. All kinds of people were coming to this wonderful God blessed country to find a better life. My husband was one of many. I shook my head and whispered, "God bless this wonderful country. May all who come here achieve the desires of their heart as they contribute to making this a truly harmonious multi-cultural society."

As the arrival time for Tony's aircraft drew nearer and nearer, I began to feel butterflies in my stomach. I constantly looked at my watch as the minutes now seemed like hours. Finally, I heard through the loudspeaker that his flight had landed. The time that I waited for him to check-out through customs and arrive at the arrival gate, seemed like eternity! To this day, I can't understand how come I did not develop strabismus of one or both eyes. I haven't experienced excitement to that extreme to this day. I don't think that at my age my heart could stand up to it!

At long last Tony appeared from around the bend leading from the customs area to the arrival gate. I made a dash to meet him. I must have flattened everyone in my path to get to my beloved Tony. As I raced towards him with open arms, he pushed the trolley with his luggage as fast as he could to get to me. It was a feeling of heaven on earth. Finally, he emerged from behind the barrier that separated us and we both hugged each other so very tightly, we almost squeezed every last drop of oxygen from our lungs. We must have stayed clung together for some time before we could release the bear hug! I looked into his eyes and saw, for the very first time during the time that I knew him, tears in his eyes! Tears of utter joy, I hasten to add. I could not control the well of tears in my eyes; I just let them flow down my cheeks. I thought to myself, if I could capture this moment and immortalise it so that I could always embrace it at will, I would. Still lost in a world which seemed at that point in time occupied by only two people, Tony and me, we began to walk towards the car driver who was waiting patiently a short distance away. I really appreciated him standing back and giving Tony and me that much required space.

Tony greeted him in his well-spoken Jamaican accent, and we were off to the multi-storey car park. We arrived at the car park and Tony's luggage was loaded into the trunk of the car. We both sat in the back seat so closely together;

one could find it very difficult to slide a hair between us! We chatted happily along the journey home. Tony told me all about his flight. He was very excited as this was the very first time that he had flown. The only thing that he complained of was the clogging up of his ears. He really thought that he would not be able to hear properly again! I re-assured him that it was only a temporary condition which was very common when one flies, and that it would not be long before he would be able to hear normally. He smiled sweetly, rubbed his ears, and replied, "OK, if you say so."

As we drove along he was fascinated by the houses. "My God," he remarked, "all the houses look the same!" Turning to me he asked, "How do you find you way around? This is incredible, and apart from looking the same, they are all joined together. This is a nightmare, and the shops, he continued, they all look the same!" He could not get over the fact that fruits were being sold from inside a shop instead of in an open market. They are called greengrocer's I informed him. "Greengroceries?" he remarked. "Why not just call them fruit stalls?" He laughed so much he had to hold on to his tummy. "I can see that I am going to encounter some language problems in England" he went on.

"Don't worry man, you soon get used to it," replied the driver. "When me come here me feel like a right idiot for the first few weeks. Everything the white people them say, sound like double-dutch to me. Me say 'no' when me should say 'yes' and when me should say 'yes please', me say 'no thank-you'! One thing me must tell you before me forget, the white people them like you if say 'please' and 'thank you.' If you want to get on in this country, don't forget your 'please' and 'thank-you'. Miss G will have to break you into the habit."

I interrupted, "Don't worry, I will." Tony seemed a bit apprehensive, as if to say, "What have I let myself in for? Have I done the right thing coming to England?"

Finally we arrived home. As Tony alighted from the car, he did a right-about turn, scanning the neighbourhood with a somewhat disappointed look on his face. I could tell there and then that he did not think much of England; at least he didn't think much of the buildings. He screwed his face up then tried to smile when I asked him if he was alright. We unloaded his luggage and entered into the house where I lived, his first remark was, "No carpet on the floor? I thought the floors would be covered with carpet as thick as a plank!" We made our way up the stairs to my room. I opened the door and entered in. His eyes bulged, his mouth opened wide with surprise. "Is this where you live?" he asked. "You live in one room?" He literally dropped the suitcase onto the floor, and stood motionless as if in shock. He stared around the room, still in a state of shock, he said, "I don't believe that my wife left a beautiful house, with a lovely garden, complete with maid, to come and live in one room. Why didn't you send and tell me," he went on.

"I know that if I had send and tell you the living conditions in England you would not have come," I replied. I tried to change the subject. "Would you like a cup of tea?" I asked.

"Tea, this time of day?" he replied. "Darling, have you gone crazy?" he continued. "I know that English people are mad, but I did not expect you to join the gang so soon after coming here," he replied.

"It is nothing to do with madness," I replied. "In the winter months, a cup of tea is the one thing that keeps you warm. You will see. Soon you will be drinking tea by the gallon like the rest of us, mark my words."

"I will have a cup of coffee, but not tea," he replied with a robust laugh.

I turned towards the door, "Would you like to come and see the kitchen?" I asked.

"Sure," he replied. We went down the stairs to the kitchen. "My God," this is a very small kitchen," he exclaimed. He nearly fainted when I told him how many people shared that tiny kitchen. He wanted to know if it was the same everywhere or if it was only that particular house that was overcrowded. I told him that it was the same story everywhere, and some places were even more overcrowded! At that point I thought it was a good time to give him the run down on the routine of how to use the kitchen, and the bathroom; especially the bathroom as I anticipated him starting work soon.

Coffee made, we went up the stairs to my one-bedroom apartment, which is a bedroom, dining-room and living room, all in one! I was very fortunate to have the largest room in the house; all the other rooms were much smaller. There was one room which was so small, called a 'box room', one could not swing a cat in it, and that was occupied by two people. I wanted to get it into Tony's head how very fortunate I was to be living in the front room. As soon as the occupants of the box room came in from work, I knocked on their door to introduce Tony to them. It was not a case of being eager for the introduction, but a case of showing him the size of the room in which two adults have to live, thus making him appreciate how lucky we were.

I had booked a week's holiday off work to enable me to show Tony around as much as I could, and also to take him to be registered with my family doctor, taking him to be registered at the exchange (the office where you put your name down for the purpose of finding work). That was what it was called in the 60s. Now it is called the unemployment office. The one place that I made sure to take Tony was Brixton market. He could not believe his eyes when I showed him around Brixton market! He was overwhelmed with excitement. He told me that for one split second he had to pinch himself to make sure that he was not in a Spanish Town market. "Well," I told him, when you want Jamaican produce you know where to go." The visit to Brixton made Tony's day, as the saying goes. He just could not stop talking about Brixton market. From then on, whenever I wanted some Jamaican produce that I could not get locally, Tony would remark, "Why didn't you go to Brixton and get it? You know that you would be sure to get it in Brixton market!"

After Tony had completed his familiarization period, it was time to look for work. We had no doubt that he would be able to find work in his profession as an accountant. Sadly, this was not the case. After attending several interviews, it was beginning to dawn on both of us that it was not easy for him to get into this field. It had got to the point where he was thinking seriously of going back home to Jamaica. He was told by the company for which he worked for several years before he came to England that if he could not find the streets of gold as the saying goes, he would be welcomed back to his job.

He became very frustrated and depressed. With all his years of experience as an accountant, no one was willing to employ him in this field. Some of the people who conducted the interviews told him point blank that there were plenty of jobs available with London transport as bus drivers, bus conductors, or to work on the underground! He found it very hard to accept that such prejudice existed on such a wide scale. Soon he began to take notice that the majority of the workforce on the buses and on the underground, were coloured!

Finally, he had to face reality. He was not going to get a job as an accountant, and he did not have the money to pay his return fare home. Apart from those two factors, people who came to England and returned home, were laughed at, and people made fun of them. They would taunt them with, "So you come back to the Rock, what happen? You never find that the streets in England were paved with gold?" The news of the person's return would spread like wild-fire, and everybody would be on the look-out for such a person, and when they caught up with them they would give them a very rough time. It was not a very pleasant situation to find one-self in! Tony thought about it and decided to swallow his pride and applied to London Transport as a last resort for the job of a bus conductor. This was very hard for him.

I loved my husband very much, but I must admit that he was a very cocky type of person. He would walk around his office with no less than three pens, and a pencil in his milk-white short-sleeved shirt pocket, left hand in trouser pocket, as he was left-handed, his feet hardly touched the ground, as he walked on air as my senior sister described his walk, which was also the description of him by many people, old and young alike! Shoes so shiny one could use them as a looking-glass (mirror). It was a great climb-down, from that way of life to working as a bus conductor! I did my best to cheer his spirit up by telling him that he could move up from conducting to becoming an Inspector.

Needless to say when he attended the interview, he was successful. He started work as a bus conductor, which was not by choice, but was compulsory. He gradually learned to accept his plight, as he found several people working with London Transport in the same situation as himself. Many of the fellows told him that they don't care about people making fun of them when they return. They were only working with the Transport until they saved up their fare and then they would be going back home.

The wages were quite good, and on top of that he would work lots of overtime, which pushed his wages even higher. After a short time, Tony bought his first car. I never forget the excitement as he drove home in his brand new Ford Anglia, dark red in colour, registration number, BLU 207B. I have a photograph of that little car until today. I treasure it very much. It is very precious. That little car brought back some esteem to Tony's life, and put some spring back into his steps. He was always a lover of cars. He was like a child with a new toy. He treated that car with such loving tender care. Very much the same as he treated his car which he had back home. Some of his friends were very happy for him, and some were very jealous! I was among the happy ones. At least now I don't have to try too hard to cheer up Tony. The responsibility is now shared between his new car and me!

Within a few days of acquiring our new car, I noticed a very dramatic change in the attitude of our landlady. Unfortunately, it was a change for the worse! She hardly spoke to us. Once she passed me in the dining room and deliberately bumped into me, then shouted, "It seems like the dining room getting too small for the both of us!" I was completely stunned at her behaviour. I began to feel very nervous, and tried not to go to the dining-room or to the kitchen when they were occupied by her. This was not easy, as all the occupants more or less got up for work at the same time, and returned home the same time; except for Tony as he did shift work. At first I did not tell Tony, but then things got so bad that I had to tell him. He told me to try and put up with the situation until we were able to find alternative accommodation.

We started the gruelling task of looking for a room, which was the term used in those days. We soon found out that it was not very easy finding a room to rent. Vacant rooms were advertised in shop windows, on small cards or pieces of paper, or pieces of cardboard. The person advertising their vacant rooms would pay a small fee to the shop owner to place their advert in the window for a period of one week. If, at the end of the week the room is not taken, they would then advertise for a further week. There were several conditions attached to one finding a vacant room. I was amazed to find conditions such as, NO COLOURED, NO CHILDREN, NO PETS, SINGLE MEN ONLY, or SINGLE WOMEN ONLY! We had not mentioned to the landlady that we were intending to vacate her front room, but it was as though she smelled a rat (she had a feeling that we were planning to leave). She now started to pick on Tony. She would sit up and wait for him to come home when on late shift. Then, when he started climbing the stairs leading up to our room, she would open her room door and shout at him, "Tek off you shoes when you come in late hours and no wake me up [Take-off your shoes when you come in so late and don't wake me up]."

Tony was so upset, he was nearly in tears. "Imagine, I leave my big house in Jamaica, although it was rented, it was ours, to come to England to live in one room and as if that is not bad enough, for people to be taking liberty with me!" That night we hardly slept.

The days following, Tony took off his shoes as soon as he came through the door and climbed the stairs in his socks! During this time we were room hunting frantically. We would comb the area during the evenings looking at adverts in shop windows. We also asked friends to enquire for us, and as you know, word gets around very fast.

What would push us to take any kind of room until we got what we wanted, was one night Tony came in late, he took his shoes off as usual and crept up the stairs. As soon as he shut the door, there was a knock. He opened the door to find the landlady standing at the door in her nightdress and dressing-gown, she shouted, "When you come in this hours of the night, no walk up and down over me head. You have money fi buy new car, you can go buy house fi put you wife in, or the two a you can go live ina the car! [If you have got money to afford to buy a new car, you can afford to buy a home for you and your wife, or both of you can go and live in the car]. I was so upset, I cried for almost the whole of the night. "Tony, we will have to find a room and move from this place by next week," I sobbed, "I can't take any more of this woman's behaviour."

That night, or perhaps I should say early morning, because I had sat up most of the night crying. I knelt down at my bedside and prayed. "God, it seems as though it is not easy to find a room, but your word says, "With man this is impossible, but not with God, for with God all things are possible," so please find us a room by next weekend. After I prayed, I felt a great peace in my soul, and I knew then that my prayers were going to be answered! We got into bed, cuddled each other for comfort, and went off to sleep.

The following day a friend came to visit and told us that there was a vacant room not far from where we were living, but they didn't know whether we would like it. Tony and I decided to go and have a look at it anyway. On arrival to the address I noticed that the house was three storeys high. My first thought was, "I hope the room is not on the third floor! I don't fancy climbing three flights of stairs." We rang the doorbell and were greeted by a middle-aged West Indian lady with a broad smile. "Hello," she said. "Can I help you?"

"We hear that you have a room to rent," I replied."

"Come in," she said. "Have you got any children?" she asked.

"No," I replied.

"OK," I will show you the room." I was taken aback to find that instead of going up the stairs, she turned around and opened a door to her right, which revealed a flight of steps leading down. Down and down we went until she finally came to the bottom of the steps, which was quite dark. She opened a door which revealed the vacant room. It had a scary feeling, it was a though the room was some feet underground! I looked at Tony, Tony looked at me with amazement, as though to say, "What the hell is this underground, or hell on earth?" She showed us around the room which was quite spacious, and fairly well decorated. She then pointed to a locked door across from that room, and told us that another tenant lived in there. A single man she went on. She then showed us the kitchen which had its own gas meter. "You have to punch your own gas," she said. "It takes six-penny pieces. I don't allow anyone to cook in their rooms on their paraffin heater," she went on.

"I had no idea that people cooked in their room on their heater." I replied with a look of surprise. She then went up the stairs to the second floor to show as around the bathroom and the toilet. You can work it out for yourself the distance one has travel to use the toilet and the bathroom, and the predicament one would find oneself in should one need to use the toilet in a hurry! There was no dining-room. There was a small table in the room with two chairs, which told us that we had to eat in our room.

At the end of the tour, I could see that she was quite keen to have Tony and me as her tenants. "Well, you like the room?" she asked.

I looked at Tony and he quickly replied, "Yes, it's OK."

"Well you can move in as soon as you like, the rent is three pounds fifty per week, plus one month's rent in advance, and when you're ready to move, you have to give me one month's notice, or you lose your deposit!" Tony took out his wallet, and handed her the money. She gave him a receipt, and two keys to the front door, and the keys to the room. She shook both our hands, she was extremely happy. Before I left my curiosity got the better of me, and I just had to ask her, "How come those two rooms and kitchen were underground?"

She burst out into a fit of laughter, which came from the very bottom of her belly! "Is this the first time you see a basement flat?"

"Yes," I replied.

"You have a lot to learn about this country," she replied, still laughing. By this time she laughed so much, tears were running down her cheeks. "Many of the houses are built like this. Down there is called the basement, and then there are some with a room at the very top, which is called the attic room," she went on to explain.

As soon as we were out of the house and turned the corner Tony and I could hardly contain ourselves. We had so much to say about our prospective home. One, we really don't like the place; it is not our cup of tea as the saying goes. In other words, it is not somewhere that we would willingly choose to live. Two, I could foresee that it would be very cold in the winter months being so deep underground, and three, the distance we had to travel to use the bathroom and the toilet! There was one good point, which was that the kitchen, although very small, was to be shared by only one other person! Suddenly, a thought came into my mind. *I hope this gentleman was not one of those people who waited until other people punched the gas, and then started cooking without punching the gas meter!* I have heard stories many times about that kind of behaviour! *Well,* I told myself, *I will just have to wait and see!*

As soon as we got back home, we started to make plans for moving on the Friday. The rent week runs from Friday to Friday, therefore, we wanted to be out by Friday. I told my family butcher, greengrocer (the shop where I purchased my fruits and vegetables), my local grocer and the milkman, that I would be moving on the Friday. They were sorry to see me go, but when I told them a bit about my predicament, they just wished me good luck. We moved out midday on the Friday before the landlady came home from work. We left her keys in the room door, and left her a note to say, "Gone to live in our new car!"

After unpacking our few personal belongings, we settled in very nicely. I was not particularly happy with the environment, but made up my mind to give it my best shot! It did not take me very long to find out that the house was very overcrowded with both adults and children. People went in and out through the front door in droves. I could not help but wonder where they all slept!

Within a short time, my worst fears became a reality. The gentleman who lived in the room across the hall from us would wait quietly in his room and, as soon as Tony or I punched the gas meter, which as I said before took sixpenny pieces, he would dash out of his room and start cooking! The first time it happened, I could not believe what I was seeing. I thought, well, perhaps he had punched the gas before we did, and did not start to cook immediately! I could not ask him if he did or did not, because I did not check the meter before I punched. Therefore, I could not say what the reading on the meter was. Tony and I decided to make a note of the meter reading before and after we punched. Yes, you guessed right, that man had the gall to come out of his room and started cooking as soon as he heard the sixpenny pieces drop in the gas meter. I decided that enough was enough! As soon as he came out and took his pot from out of the cupboard, I confronted him very nicely and calmly, "I did not hear you punch the gas meter," I said.

"Yes man, me punch the gas," he replied.

"No, you did not" I answered. "Before I punched the meter, it was reading… and it is still reading…" I said! Well, he was so ashamed. He started to laugh. "I could swear I did punch the gas,s" he continued. "Never mind, next time me will punch!"

I could not help but wonder what have we had let ourselves in for! A lot of people complained about people who would sit quietly in their rooms and wait to hear when others dropped their sixpences in the gas meter to enable them to obtain gas for the purpose of cooking their meals, and then these people would creep out of their rooms and start cooking. Sometimes the person who punched the meter would not complete cooking their meals before the gas ran out, and they had to punch again, and the person who did not punch, would have the nerve to continue cooking as if nothing had happened!

This man's bad habit became a regular occurrence! The problem was that he was a very nice person. One with whom you could not really have a quarrel. When he was caught using gas that he hadn't punched, he would just laugh and say something funny, which made me or Tony laugh instead of becoming cross with him. I decided that it was an expensive laugh and told the landlady about it, and asked her to have a word with him nicely. She did, and guess what? He started cooking in his room on his paraffin heater, which is meant for one purpose, to keep the room warm in the winter months. It was hard to believe someone could be so mean! Finally, he was caught out by the landlady when she had occasion to enter his room, and noticed that the ceiling in his room was black with the smoke from the paraffin heater, and that the room had a smell of cooking!

We were living there for a short period, when he told us that his wife was joining him from Jamaica. Although I was happy for both him and his wife because of the experience that I had living away from my husband for a period of

time, I did not know whether I would be able to cope with
another person sharing that tiny kitchen! Then a second
thought crept into my mind, perhaps when she joins him
she will be able to persuade him to punch his own gas when
he needs to do any cooking and stop using ours!

Finally, his wife joined him. He introduced her to Tony
and me. She appeared to be a very calm, quiet lady. I soon
found out that she was a Christian. Hence, the reason for
her calm, quiet character.

The first few days after her arrival were almost a
nightmare, due to the fact that both of them would be
occupying the kitchen at the same time! Apart from the
kitchen becoming more crowded, so was the gas cooker
as she tended to cook a number of dishes. She would wait
for him to come in from work before she started to cook
because she was not familiar with the gas cooker!

You are not going to believe this, but instead of his
wife persuading him to punch the gas meter, somehow the
situation remained the same! By this time, I had become
quite frustrated. I did not want to say anything to the wife
about the situation for the simple reason that I did not want
her to feel that I was picking on her. Apart from that, due to
the fact that she had only just arrived in the country, I did
not want to be the first person to make her feel unhappy.
The only course of action was that whenever I cornered the
husband on his own, I would remind him nicely to punch
the gas when he and his wife needed to cook. Sometimes it
worked, and sometimes it didn't.

Just as we were trying not to let this unreasonable
situation get on our nerves, another cropped up! Suddenly
we were unable to sleep at night. The landlady would stay

up until the early hours of the morning sewing. She took items from a factory which she would make up using a very powerful industrial sewing machine, and her bedroom was immediately above ours. At first when it started, Tony and I were dumbfounded, so was the other couple. One could not believe that one could be so inconsiderate to others! She would start her sewing around ten o'clock at night and carried on until four o'clock in the morning! All that time Tony and I could only toss and turn in our bed! Sometimes he would swear, turn on the light, jump out of bed and say "I am going upstairs to tell that damn woman, landlady or no landlady, I want to sleep because I and my wife have to go to work in the morning." I would manage to calm him down with encouraging statements such as "Don't mind, my dear, God will help us to find somewhere suitable to live one day." With that and a hot cup of Ovaltine or milk, he would get back into bed, turn off the light and wait for the racket to stop.

We were nearly driven mad with that power machine. Eventually one night Tony jumped out of bed, switched the light on and checked the clock; it was three o'clock in the morning! I could see that by the mood he was in, that no amount of Ovaltine, milk, or sweet talking from me, was going to stop him from going upstairs to tell the landlady to have some consideration for us and the other couple who were also suffering sleepless nights. He put on his dressing gown and bed slippers and stormed out the door. He went up the stairs, knocked on her door and told her to switch off the damn machine so that he and his wife and the other couple could get some sleep!

I could hear the landlady shouting, but could not hear clearly what she was saying. After a barrage of exchange of sharp words, Tony returned to the room. I asked him what the landlady was shouting about. I was astonished to hear that she had said that it is her house, and she can do what she damn well pleased, and no tenant is going to tell her what to do in her own house. Tony was in a state of utter devastation, and so was I. Here we were in a foreign country, stripped of property, possession, and a way of life that we were accustomed to, living in one room, rented from someone who we considered below our class, and sharing accommodation with people with unreasonable behaviour. We both felt a complete failure. This was almost a turning point to push us to returning home!

The following day, Tony bumped into the landlady at the front door, who told him that she would like to have a word with him at his earliest convenience. When he told me, I knew then what the word would be about. I told him that she is going to ask us to leave! The thought of finding another accommodation so soon after moving into this place was almost unbearable. The likelihood of getting another landlady with the same attitude as those we had already experienced was a reality!

That evening, Tony and I decided that he should go and see her. We had our evening meal, gave her some time to have hers, and settle down to watch T.V. That was the normal routine. He then went upstairs, knocked on her door, and waited. The door opened and she shouted at him, "Me a beg you fe come outa me room by Friday. You nah come in ya fe come tell me wa fe do! [I am asking you to leave by Friday. You are not coming in here to tell me what to do]." Tony told her, "OK no problem." I can't say that I was sorry to go; I wanted to get out of that underground hell hole!

Once more the race was on to find a room. We looked in all the local shop windows, sub-post office windows, and asked around verbally. There is a saying which goes, out of evil come forth good. The irony of that woman, made me determined to buy our own house! In the first instance we had decided to stay in this wonderful country for five years. Five years was the time limit set by almost all Jamaicans, and then they would return home to buy their own homes! I had no intention of buying a house in this country, but when I saw what my husband and I were going through with people who back home would be classed as 'lower class', they certainly would not be able to afford their own home. I thought, Tony and I will now begin to save hard towards buying our own home as from this moment. We had another four years in which to live in England, and I certainly can't continue to be moving every so often, because of house-owners who exploit people who they call just come. They tend to forget that it is the just come who are putting money in their pockets to enable them to pay the mortgage for their homes!

Finally, we were told about a lady who had a very large room to rent. Tony and I went to view the room; this time it was on the second floor of the house. There were two rooms on the same floor, and one in the attic. (The attic room is usually quite small in the highest story of the building, immediately under the ceiling.) They are usually very cold in the winter months, and very hot in the summer months. They are usually rented at a much cheaper rate. A lovely couple lived in the room next to the one we were hoping to rent, and a young man lived in the attic room. The small kitchen was to be shared by all parties.

Luck was on our side, at least for the time being. We got the room. It was the usual routine, of X amount of rent in advance, and the laying down of the laws. We also had to punch our own gas for cooking purposes etc. We were fairly comfortable living there. One thing that really upset me was that, when the gasman came and emptied the gas meter, the landlady would come up into our kitchen, and take the rebate money. I don't know how it works, but usually when the gas-board clears the meter, they would leave behind some money, which the person who was responsible for punching the meter, would collect. The amount would then be written on the gas-meter card. Sometimes, it would be quite a substantial amount, depending on how much gas one punches during the three-monthly period. The first time she confiscated the money, I was quite shocked! She had her meter downstairs in her apartment, the rebate of which she kept, and then had the gall to come up the stairs into the tenant's kitchen, and take their rebate as well! I asked the other lady if that had always been the case, to which she replied, "It has been this way since we lived here!" Although I was very upset about it, I was afraid to confront her about the mater, just in case she asked us to get out of her house. That was the way house-owners usually give notice to quit! Tony and I decided to let her get away with it. We came to the conclusion that a few sixpenny pieces would not make us rich! So we decided to "grin and bear it" as the saying goes.

During our time of living there, I received a letter from Jamaica to say that my brother was in the process of coming to England, and could I find him a room. God was on my side, just across the road from where I lived, I was told that a room was up for rent. I quickly went across to see the landlady, made the necessary down-payments, and secured the room for my brother. I informed my landlady that my brother would be coming over, and that from time to time he would be visiting me, as I would be cooking his meals for him. I was horrified when she told me that I had to pay her key money, I had to pay her five shillings per week to enable me to give my brother a key to the front door to visit me! There was nothing that I could do about it. It was a case of take it, or leave it!

Tony and I were more determined to buy our own home within the not too distant future. He worked several hours of overtime to make up his wages, which enabled us to save a substantial amount each week, and was still able to pay the rent and other bills quite comfortably. Food on the whole, including dry goods, such as rice, sugar and flour, was very cheap. Clothes and shoes cost a fraction of the price that we were used to paying back home, which contributed to the speed in which we were able to build up our savings.

Before long, we started to look around and to check out the price of houses. I had a pleasant surprise when I found out how cheap houses were! One could get a three bedroomed house for as little as two thousand pounds! The mortgage repayments were also quite cheap. I was also surprised to find that on most occasions the houses would be sold with some furniture, including piano, in good condition at no extra cost. A friend of ours, who bought her house during the time that we were looking around, told me that she bought her three-bedroom house for less than two thousand pounds, almost fully furnished, including a grand piano in excellent condition!

During our house price checking out period, I had a surprise which was not so pleasant! I found out that most white people would not sell their homes to black people, no matter how much they offered. They would make up all kinds of excuses and apply delaying tactics to put off the black would-be buyer!

It wasn't long before we found what we thought was the ideal home; a three-bedroom house in a very quiet part of South East London, complete with a very large and beautiful English garden, including roses, which are my favourite flowers. In the middle of the garden was a pear tree which produced fruits as the stars! There were also two apple trees; one cox's apple and one cooking apple. Those also produced lots of fruits. One half of the garden was laid to lawn. I was very proud of my perfect English garden. Before we decided to buy that house, we could have got a three-storey house with six bedrooms for just over three thousand pounds; I did not like it as I thought that it was too big! Tony also said he didn't want such a large house. We thought that a small three-bedroom house was more stylish. If I knew then, what I know today, I would have grabbed that house with both arms!

We went ahead and completed the purchase of our dream three-bedroom home, not too far from my new found friend, who I met in the laundromat. In the 60s some areas had very few black people as residents, and one felt comfortable when one met another black person. When I met that lady, we got chatting about back home, and the conditions with which we had to cope with here in England. We exchanged addresses, and telephone numbers. The friendship developed very quickly, as I was happy to find someone with which I could relate. Before long, I invited her and her husband around, and the two husbands became great friends. We were like one big happy family! We had so much in common.

The most exciting thing about owning my very own home was when Tony and I went shopping for furniture and other household items! I wanted to buy the very best. As a matter of fact, I did buy the very best, including carpet on my stairs, which I had never experienced before. A thick-piled carpet for my living room and beautiful pink carpet for the bedrooms. I felt like a queen! It was a really good feeling. I had to pinch myself to make sure that I was not dreaming. After a very short time in this blessed country, I was the proud owner of a new car and a beautifully furnished home. All glory and honour be to my God who saw what injustice my husband and I suffered at the hands of landladies.

After we had settled in our newly acquired home, it was time for re-decorating. Of course, I had to buy the most expensive wallpaper. It was a matter of no expense spared, and Tony was with me all the way! He would just say, "Only the best is good enough for my wife." We set about decorating the complete house. It was weeks of putting up with inconvenience, as everything was piled up in the middle of the rooms, and covered over. Sometimes, it was almost impossible to get to things, but we were determined to see it through. Tony was one of those men, who God had blessed with several talents. He could do almost anything! He could paint, hang wallpaper, lay carpet and lino, lay tiles, fix curtain rails and he even went up on the roof and replaced broken tiles! I was very fortunate to be married to him. The house was owned by an old white lady who had died, and because of that factor it was not in good decorative condition. Hence the fact that it needed a lot of refurbishment to bring it into line with our requirements. I am proud to say that we did not have to pay out one penny to do the work Tony did it all!

It took quite a while for the work to be completed, but when it eventually did, it was quite a sight to behold! At last I was able to fix my furniture, and other household fixtures, in their places. It was time for Tony and me to celebrate. We invited our friends round and had a lovely meal, cooked in my own kitchen, shared only with the Spirit of God who is always with me. For the first time since I arrived in England, I felt like a real lady (the way that I am accustomed to feel). Complete freedom to do what I want to do, when I want to do it, without confrontation.

My newfound joy in my 'ideal home' was short-lived, as I gradually came to the conclusion that the house was haunted! I spent a great deal of time alone in the house when Tony was on shift work.

It all started one day as I was in the kitchen cooking. I heard what sounded like a large group of people laughing at the top of the stairs! The laughter echoed much the same as when I was a young child back home. My father rented a piece of land from a rich white landowner which climbed up to the top of a high hill. My brother and I would play a game wherein one of us would climb up the top of the hill and shout, "Hello," to the one in the valley. The echo of our voices would travel a very long way, and sounded muffled. We were fascinated by the sound of the echo, and would spend a very long time on the hill repeating the 'hello and listen to the echo' saga! Sometimes, we would get carried away and lose all track of time. On our arrival home, we would be confronted by our father, who would ask in his usual angry tone of voice, "Why the hell were you two shouting at the top of your voices, 'hello,' hello', and creating such a commotion?"

When I first heard the laughter, I did not want to believe it. I was extremely frightened, and to make matters worse, I was alone in the house! I stopped what I was doing and listened for a while. The laughter seemed to get louder, and louder! I came out of the kitchen and stood at the bottom of the stairs and looked up. What sounded like a group of people standing at the top of the stairs burst out in laughter! It was as though 'they' were laughing at me. It was very scary. What made it even scarier was I could feel the presence of those 'people' so very real, but could not see them! As the laughter got louder, and louder, the echo filled the whole house. I stood at the bottom of the stairs looking up, for quite a while. I suppose I wanted to make sure that I was not hearing things. 'They' just carried on laughing, and the echo of the laughter got louder, and louder! The experience was so real, it was awful! When I was convinced that it was really happening, I dashed out of the house, and stood at the gate, with the front door ajar. By this time, I was shaking with fright. I could not bring myself to go back into that house!

I must have stood at the gate for hours! Finally, Tony drove up from work. I was so very glad to see him. "What are you doing out here, with the front door wide open?" he asked. He could see that I was frightened. He held my hand, and we both went in. By this time the laughter had stopped, and everything was as normal. He led me into the front room (sitting room), and sat me down. "Come on tell me what happened," he asked, with a look of concern on his face. I told him the story. He did not appear too surprised, which made me wonder if he had some kind of experience before and did not tell me, as knowing him, he would not want to frighten me. "Oh don't worry about it," he replied "Maybe the old lady doesn't like black people!" With that said, he started to laugh. That must have been the first time that Tony laughed at his own joke all by himself, as I could not see the funny side of the joke. That was the beginning of many more of those laughing sagas! They now happened on a regular basis, always when I was alone in the house, and always at the same spot at the top of the stairs.

My ideal home became a living hell! It had gotten to the point where I dreaded the moment when Tony kissed me goodbye as he went off to work. It was as though 'they' were watching, and waiting for him to go off to work, so that 'they' could start their laughing ritual!

To put the icing on the cake as the saying goes, one night I dreamt that Tony and I were sitting in the sitting room, which is to the front of the house. An old white lady appeared at the window, holding a handful of grass. She threw the grass through the window, which actually landed over both Tony and I! She then shouted, "Get out of my house!" That dream explained the mysterious phenomenon laughing saga! I told Tony to put the house up for sale. It was with a very sorrowful heart that I arrived at that conclusion, but I could not continue to live in that house. It had become a living hell. The house was put up for sale, and was snapped up very quickly, because it was very well decorated, with beautiful fitted carpets throughout. I don't know what experience the new occupiers had, because to this day, I never as much as walk pass that house.

I can never forget the winters of the 1960s. The snow would fall so hard during the nights; I would wake up the following morning to find that Tony or I had to reach for the shovel to clear some of the snow away from the front door, before we could venture out. The snow would be knee deep. Although I would wear thick winter coats, gloves, scarves, cardigans (sweater), woolly hats, winter boots and socks, not forgetting the long-johns (long warm bloomers with elastic in the legs), which clung to my legs" – this was on top of the normal knickers (panties) and I would still be freezing! I had suffered several falls as I slipped on the snow. One would slip and slide onto one's back, ending up quite a distance from the initial fall. Several people would suffer broken bones falling in the snow. Thank God I never had a broken bone, although I suffered several bruises!

One would wake up in the morning and could not distinguish between one house and the other. They would be completely covered over with snow. They reminded me of a row of cotton trees with all the pods bursting open!

Then there was the Mr. Frost! The frost would cause my hands to suffer a burning sensation. It doesn't matter how thick the gloves are, the frost would penetrate them, and it doesn't matter how thick the socks were, Mr Frost would penetrate them, causing a condition of the feet called chilblains. This was so painful, one could hardly walk.

Next was the dreaded fog, the black fog would be so dense that one could not see three feet in front of one's eyes! This awful thick black fog would find its way up the nostrils, and when I blew or wiped my nose, it would be pitch black. The fog would be so thick that I and others would be walking like blind people, taking slow steps. Sometimes people would bump into each other, as they could not see clearly. On several occasions I would go past my bus stop because of the fog. I can remember once the black fog was so bad, that I had to walk and feel along the walls. I was very scared. The irony was that, one moment the day would be quite bright, and the next moment it would be pitch black! Midday would suddenly be plunged into pitch darkness, as though it was midnight! Sometimes it was a case of four seasons in one day, instead of four seasons in the year!

People would clasp their palms around a mug or cup of hot tea instead of holding it by the handle to try to keep their hands warm. It was a matter of tea, and more tea! I would drink so much tea that I noticed that my teeth were getting black! I did not realize that it was caused by the volume of tea that I was drinking, until I went to the dentist and asked him to pull out my teeth as they were getting bad and to replace them with dentures! He gave me a good telling off. "You stupid girl, you want me to pull out your good teeth!" He then told me that I was drinking too much tea, which was causing my teeth to go black!

I was deeply amazed at the way that the white people loved their dogs and cats. They are not called a nation of animal lovers for nothing. The first time that I saw a white lady walking her dog in the snow dressed in winter warmers (a coat made to fit the dog, and booties on the dog's feet), I stood and stared so much, she must have thought that I was staring at her, but I was staring at the dog's apparel! Shock number two was, I noticed that white people would be walking their dogs, and people would stroke the dog, and say things such as, "Hello, who is a lovely doggie?" and would completely ignore the dog's owner. Shock number three, was when I went into the supermarket and noticed the variety of canned foods for dogs and cats on display! Some poor old lady would arrive at the check-out with a shopping trolley loaded with tins of dog and cat food, but very little food stuff for herself. It was as though she did not mind going without, just as long as her dog and cat were well fed!

Here in England, dogs and cats share the home with equal rights as their owners. Cats are toilet-trained, just like a small child. They have their tray with a stuff on the tray called 'cat litter'. Whenever the cat wants to do their thing, they would go to their tray. Dogs are taken for walks at intervals, so as to enable them to open their bowels, mainly in the parks, or behind a tree by the street side. Although some dogs don't teach their bottoms any manners, and would just stop and go anywhere, by the lamppost, at someone's gate, wherever the mood took them. I would honestly say that dogs and cats are treated on equal par as children. If one wants to find oneself behind bars quickly and without much bother, just throw a small stone and hit a dog or a coat, or ill-treat them in anyway. Your feet would not touch the ground, as the saying goes back home!

When I remember how dogs and cats were treated back home, not that they were badly treated, but not with half the attention and care that the British dogs and cats are accustomed, I can't help but laugh! As a child, it was normal to throw stones at other people's dogs or cats if they ventured into one's yard, and as to sharing the home, that was only done at meal-times. The dog or cat was allowed to come in and sit looking up at the family having their meals, who would then throw them some of the food. That's as far as they were privileged in regards to sharing the house.

As a small child my father had a dog called Captin. Although he was much loved by my parents, and all the children, his bedroom was a cardboard box lined with old clothing, which was kept in a small outhouse where my father stored yams, coffee beans and coco-pods!

I congratulate the English for their sincere love of dogs and cats, and animals of all types. I will then say to the dogs, cats and all other animals, who are British citizens, "You don't know how very lucky you all are!" Make sure that you don't even think about immigrating to Jamaica. If you do, you can expect to be treated in a way that you are not accustomed to! In plain language, you will be pretty much in the same situation that I and other immigrants found ourselves in when we first arrived in this Great Motherland! Take the advice of someone who knows what she is talking about. These two words sum it up in a nutshell! STAY HERE!

There is something else that I still can't get used to after spending almost forty years in this God-blessed country, and that is, children calling adults by their Christian names! As soon as the child is able to speak, they begin to call adults by their Christian names. Even if the adult is one hundred years old, a toddler who is just learning to talk, calls the old person by their first name, and that is normal. Even now, this week, I was out in my garden, and my neighbour's grandson, who is approximately five years old, shouted, "Hello Gloria!" It is completely normal practice. The very first time that I heard a small child call an adult by their first name, I was horrified!

I thought that the child was very naughty and waited for the mother to say something. I could not believe it when she said nothing. After that incident, I noticed that all the children did that, regardless of whether they were white or mixed-race, or West Indians, or whatever. It gradually dawned on me that is how it is in England!

When I was a child back home the thought of calling adults by their first name would not enter my head, because it was just not done! Even in regards to my elder sisters and brothers, I was not allowed to call them by their first names. I had to say, Sister Ethlin, Sister Roslyn, Brother William, Brother Franklin, and so on.

Another foreign behaviour that I could not help but notice was the way that children answer back when spoken to by their parents! The smallest of children, as long as they can speak, would answer back when spoken to by their parents, mothers especially. Some little ones would even go as far as to slap their mothers and what would mummy do? Just laugh and jokingly say to the child, "Don't do that." Of course, the child would reply with giving mummy another slap! As a child growing up in my day answering back was not heard of! Slap mum or dad! Not even in one's dream! That was not in the book of growing up in those days.

I strongly do believe in the saying, 'charity beings at home', and the material for making a good citizen begins at home, at a very early age. My father had a saying, two sayings as a matter of fact. One, "You can't bend the tree when it is old," and two, "It is no good shutting the gate when the mule already gone through." I thank God every day for the way that I and my brothers and sisters were brought up. It made us all better men and women today.

Whatever time I go home to Jamaica for holidays, I usually stay with a brother of mine, and it has now become part of the holiday package, that ever so often we will sit on the veranda, until late, just reflecting on our childhood days.

My brother lives in the town, which is a completely different way of life from the people who live in the country. He has two sons who still live at home, and I would say they have life very easy. I would sit along with my brother, and other family members, and tell them what our childhood was like! They would laugh and say, "Auntie, I don't believe it." Sometimes the reply would be, "Not me." The 'going back in time conversation' wold become so real, it was as though it all happened yesterday!

I almost forgot to mention something that I could not understand initially when I came to England in the early 60s. I would notice that white young men, and young ladies, but mainly the young men, would be wearing a watch, but they would still come up to me, smile, and ask me if I could tell them the time! At first, I thought, "Well perhaps their watch was not working," then I noticed that it happened very often, several times in one day. I would be walking along, and they would approach me, smile and ask for the time, still wearing a watch. I got quite fed up with this, and decided to ask someone who had been in England for a while, why this was. They laughed and told me that, there is a saying among some of the white people, especially the younger ones, that in the West Indies, we don't need a watch or a clock to tell the time, we tell the time by looking up at the sun. Asking the time is a way of teasing the coloured people. The next person who asked me the time, after I was told the reason for this, each time I was asked the time, I gave an appropriate answer! Eventually all the 'just come' as new arrivals were called, got smart to the 'have you got the time' saga.

I have seen Great Britain change culturally, socially and spiritually, over the past thirty nine years beyond my wildest dreams!

No longer do I have to travel miles to Brixton Market to buy my native food produce. I only have to take a short walk to my local supermarket! Some supermarkets have a complete area set aside, where 'exotic foods' are stocked. Apart from the supermarket, the local street markets, and most greengrocers, cater for such foods. Some shops/grocery stores, especially the Indians, stock mainly 'exotic foods!'

Sometimes I can't help but smile when I see white people, mainly women, buying yam, green bananas, sweet potatoes, mangoes, pumpkin, etc. The other day, I went to my local Indian greengrocery/grocery store, to buy my usual supply of yam, bread-fruit, sweet potatoes and pumpkin to cook my chicken soup. I was somewhat astonished when the white lady, who was behind me, took up a piece of pumpkin, examined it very carefully, and then said to me, "It's dry, isn't it?" I just smiled and said, "It is." She really knew what she was talking about, because there was more than one variety on the counter, and that was the type that I usual bought! Then, of course, she went on to buy yam, a slice of bread-fruit and a small cho-cho. I had no doubt that she too was preparing her ingredients for her chicken soup. This is a sure sign that her husband or partner is from Jamaica, or some other West-Indian country.

There is no longer a feeling of isolation. One now has a feeling of home from home, minus the sunshine, which is not a problem, as this can be over-come by going back home for holidays, to top up oneself with a good dose of sunshine at regular intervals.

I am a sunshine lover by nature, and because of my love of the sun, I have travelled to several, what I refer to as sunshine-guaranteed countries, which includes the following:

Florida
Malta
Spain (five times)
Tunisia, which includes 3 days staying in the Sahara desert
Nigeria (Africa)
Ghana (Africa)
Egypt
Israel (five times)
Germany (summer-time)
Holland
Paris
And last, but not least, lovely sunny Barbados (3 times)

During my nearly 39 years living and working in this wonderful God-blessed mother country, I have seen her change from accommodating a small number of black immigrants, to becoming a 'rainbow' country. I honestly think that I am right in saying, "There is someone living in England, from every country on the planet earth!" GREAT BRITAIN IS TRULY A MOTHER COUNTRY in the true sense of the word, and she tries her best to provide food, shelter, clothing, medical care and education for all her children, legitimate and illegitimate, alike!